CHECK YOURSELF BEFORE YOU · WRECK · YOURSELF

3 MONTH DEVOTIONAL

CHECK YOURSELF BEFORE YOU · WRECK · YOURSELF

3 MONTH DEVOTIONAL

ERIK V. SAHAKIAN

WILDWOOD IGNITED

PUBLISHING

Cover Design/Layout: Andrew Enos
Back Cover Photograph: Jocelyn Maloney

All Scripture is taken from the New King James Version
of the Bible. Copyright © 1979, 1980, 1982 by Thomas
Nelson, Inc. Used by permission. All rights reserved.

Library of Congress Control Number: 2015917642

ISBN 978-0-9852857-2-2
First Printing: November 2016

FOR INFORMATION CONTACT:

Wildwood Ignited Publishing:
A Ministry of Wildwood Calvary Chapel
35145 Oak Glen Rd
Yucaipa, CA 92399
www.wildwoodcalvary.com

Printed in the United States of America

This book is dedicated to my wife, Juanita, and my children, Skylar and Maksim, who always cheer me on and make me laugh harder than anyone else.

Acknowledgments

A special thank you to my beautiful daughter, Skylar, for helping me organize these devotionals. Sharing this experience with you was my favorite part of the writing process!

Thank you, Danielle Wingerd, for your editing skills and attention to detail.

As always, Andrew Enos, thank you for offering your creative talents to this book, but most of all your friendship and encouragement throughout all these years.

Foreword

If you know the blessing of sitting around with good friends and sharing stories about life, and lessons that you've learned, this book will feel very familiar to you. It is mostly a storybook, where God turns out to be a recurring character in all the stories. Erik is a great storyteller whose story is easy to relate to. He isn't the hero of all his own stories. Most often his stories are an honest recounting of his failures, met by the grace and faithfulness of God.

Because Erik is a father and husband, who also clearly recollects what it was like to struggle as an insecure kid, younger people will find this book easily relatable. Much of it is about marriage, childrearing, and the daily struggles of modern life. But older people will be taken back to memories and lessons from their past, and will also benefit from the wisdom of reflection.

Ultimately this devotional will help you start your day, each and every day for three months, with funny, honest truths, as God's Holy Word meets real life head on. I'm sure you will enjoy it!

Pastor Dave Rolph

Senior Pastor, Calvary Chapel Pacific Hills

Bible Teacher, *The Balanced Word* radio program

Preface

You might think that a book of devotions titled *Check Yourself Before You Wreck Yourself* is an odd choice. Though I admit that it's an unconventional title, the concept is 100% biblical.

In Second Corinthians 13:5, Paul writes, "Examine yourselves as to whether you are in the faith. Test yourselves. Do you not know yourselves, that Jesus Christ is in you?—unless indeed you are disqualified." The word for "disqualified" in the Greek is *adokimos* and it means to "not stand the test or prove oneself."

In other words, Paul was telling the church to examine themselves, test themselves, and know themselves, lest they fail the test. Or another way of saying it in our vernacular—check yourself before you wreck yourself!

One of the best ways we can "check ourselves" is through the Word of God. Hebrews 4:12 tells us "For the word of God is living and powerful...and is a discerner of the thoughts and intents of the heart." God's Word exposes us.

It's my prayer that as you read through these devotions over the next three months that God's Word will help you examine yourself. As the Word comes alive in your life, you, too, will come alive as it reveals and heals your heart.

This Book of the Law shall not depart from your mouth, but you shall meditate in it day and night, that you may observe to do according to all that is written in it. For then you will make your way prosperous, and then you will have good success.

Joshua 1:8

Day 1—Better Than Any Superhero

In my family, I was the eldest child and on the school playground I never had an "older" brother or sister to come to my defense if someone was pushing me around. In fact, I remember when I was in elementary school I often wished I had an older sibling that could come and lend me a hand when circumstances were beyond my control. Now that I think about it that may be where my fascination with real life superheroes began. I've always admired our men and women in uniform. I even applied to be a deputy sheriff and an F.B.I agent, but God in his sovereignty closed those doors. And yes, I haven't outgrown Batman and Star Wars either!

It's funny—even though I am an adult I still need a superhero to defend me. It says in First Peter 5:8, "Be sober, be vigilant; because your adversary the devil walks about like a roaring lion, seeking whom he may devour." That's a real eye-opener—to imagine our enemy actually seeking opportunities to destroy us. It's like the bully at school, scanning the playground looking for that one student to harass. Or even more accurate, the ultimate villain.

I have great news! Satan isn't the only one looking for an opportunity. It says in Second Chronicles 16:9, "For the eyes of the Lord run to and fro throughout the whole earth, to show Himself strong on behalf of those whose heart is loyal to Him." Unlike Satan, who is an inferior "created" being, our God is omniscient, meaning He knows all things, omnipresent, which means He is everywhere at once, and omnipotent, meaning He is all powerful. That means our Defender is more than capable of showing Himself strong on our behalf!

So next time you feel you need someone to stand up for you, to protect and defend you, in the midst of life's storms, remember the ultimate superhero of whom David said:

> I will love You, O Lord, my strength.
> The Lord is my rock and my fortress and
> my deliverer; my God, my strength, in
> whom I will trust; my shield and the horn
> of my salvation, my stronghold. I will
> call upon the Lord, who is worthy to be
> praised; so shall I be saved from my
> enemies. (Psalm 18:1-3)

God is better than any superhero that this world has to offer!

Day 2—Don't Grasp for the Wind

Have you ever wanted something so badly you could hardly stand it, and then once you finally got it, you realized it wasn't so special after all? I remember shortly after I began my very first job at Blockbuster Video that I saw a Millennium Falcon statue in a Star Wars magazine. I wanted it badly, but it cost around $150. Back in 1993, minimum wage was $4.25 an hour, so it took me two weeks and my entire paycheck to save up enough money to buy it. When the package finally came in the mail I excitedly tore open the box and pulled out a statue the size of my palm! What a rip off. That's what happens when you ignore the phrase "not to scale" in the full page advertisement. I remember thinking to myself, *I worked two whole weeks for this?* I ended up sending it back for a refund.

Solomon, who was the richest, wisest man of his time, experienced the same disappointment. He had pursued every pleasure and accomplishment, yet none of it satisfied. He writes in Ecclesiastes 2:11, "Then I looked on all the works that my hands had done and on the labor in which I had toiled; and indeed all was vanity and grasping for the wind. There was no profit under the sun." Have you ever tried grasping for the wind? It's an exercise in futility because it will leave you empty-handed every single time.

Contrast how Solomon felt with what Paul writes in Philippians 3:7-9, saying:

> But what things were gain to me, these I have counted loss for Christ. Yet indeed I also count all things loss for the excellence of the knowledge of Christ Jesus my Lord, for whom I have suffered the loss of all things, and count them as rubbish, that I may gain Christ and be found in Him.

Pursuing the pleasures of this world will never fully satisfy us and can often leave us feeling like we just got ripped off. The world and what it offers will never be able to meet our expectations or fulfill our needs. Jesus, on the other hand, will always satisfy us. Today, let's spend some quality time with our Savior by studying and meditating in His Word, and just conversing with Him in prayer. I guarantee we won't regret it!

Day 3—That Is in Your Job Description

When I was a young man entering the workforce for the first time, I remember my boss warning me to never be the type of employee who says, "That's not in my job description." I had never heard that phrase before and I was uncertain of its meaning. My boss explained to me that there are two types of employees: those who are willing to volunteer and take on added responsibility, to go above and beyond the call of duty, and then there are those who refuse to do anything more than what is required of them in their written job description. The latter, when directed to do certain tasks, would decline the request on the basis that it was not part of their job. Their refrain would be, "That's not in my job description." As Christians, we need to be careful that we never have that attitude toward the calling that God has placed on each of our lives.

In Acts 26:16, Paul speaks of the heavenly vision he received from Jesus Christ on the road to Damascus in which Christ says to him, "But rise and stand on your feet; for I have appeared to you for this purpose, to make you a minister and a witness both of the things which you have seen and of the things which I will yet reveal to you." Paul was called to be a minister of the gospel of Jesus Christ. Lest we think that was a calling unique only to him, consider Jesus' departing words to His disciples in Matthew 28:19-20—"Go therefore and make disciples of all the nations, baptizing them in the name of the Father and of the Son and of the Holy Spirit, teaching them to observe all things that I have commanded you."

Every Christian is called to be a minister of the gospel because we are all commanded to "go" and "make disciples." This is the Great Commission! It is the blessed responsibility of every Christian (not just a select few) to share the very same gospel with others that has brought them freedom and salvation in Christ. As Paul writes in First Corinthians 15:3-4:

> For I delivered to you first of all that which I also received: that Christ died for our sins according to the Scriptures, and that He was buried, and that He rose again the third day according to the Scriptures.

Paul delivered that which he *received*. Likewise, we must also deliver to others the gospel that we have received.

Romans 10:17 says, "So then faith comes by hearing, and hearing by the word of God." How can people hear if no one is telling them? Being ministers of the gospel is a command that is in ALL our job descriptions!

Day 4—Chillin' With Jesus

Every person is challenged by worry and anxiety in their lives. Yet, worrying does not change our circumstances and can actually cause us emotional, physical, and spiritual harm. Satan uses worrying to distract us so that we are focused more on ourselves than on God. Worrying implies that we think we are somehow in control, that we can change every circumstance, and that we are in charge. Nothing can be further from the truth! The truth is that God is in charge and we need to trust in Him. When we trust God and release our problems to Him, He will give us the peace and rest that we long for!

In Matthew 6:25-34, Jesus uses the phrase "do not worry" three times. It's pretty clear that worrying is not something that God desires for His precious children.

I remember when I was in school, the night before final exams I would stay up late, cramming as much information into my brain that I could, all the while worrying that I wasn't going to pass my tests the next day. I remember one night, my senior year, I was running through my usual playbook when I felt the Holy Spirit telling me that I had done enough worrying and it was time to find rest at the feet of Jesus. I picked up my guitar, climbed up on the roof, and had such a sweet time of worship that filled me with so much calm and peace that afterward, I immediately went to bed and fell asleep. The next day I did just fine on my exams.

Throughout the Bible, God calls on us to basically just calm down and relax. Psalm 46:10 says, "Be still, and know that I am God." Psalm 37:7 proclaims, "Rest in the Lord, and wait patiently for Him." Job 37:14 tells us to "stand still and consider the wondrous works of God." You get the idea!

Jesus said in Matthew 11:28, "Come to Me, all you who labor and are heavy laden, and I will give you rest."

So when life's problems begin to weigh us down, instead of wasting our time stressing out about stuff, let's run first to Jesus to help guide us through troubling circumstances. He's available 24/7 and no problem is too big for Him!

Day 5—A Bother or a Blessing?

Do you remember the last time you went to Disneyland or were stuck in a traffic jam? I'm sure the last thing you had hoped for in that moment was to run into that sea of endless humanity. How did it make you feel? I know when I find myself in that kind of situation I certainly struggle against my natural "fleshly" tendencies to see all those nameless masses in a negative light. Most people would probably see that ocean of strangers as a major inconvenience, perhaps even an obstacle to overcome.

But that's not how Jesus sees people! In the book of Matthew he records a scene where Jesus, after hearing about the murder of his cousin, John the Baptist, leaves for a time to be by Himself. I imagine He was saddened by John's death and wanted to be alone to spend time in prayer and reflection. However, the crowds followed Him (we later learn the crowd was numbered at 5,000 men, not including the women and children).

Imagine yourself in those shoes. You just lost a member of your family and when you try to get away for some private time, thousands of strangers follow you instead! How would you react in such a scenario? Probably *not* the way Jesus did! I am always amazed when I read about Jesus' response in

Matthew 14:14—"And when Jesus went out He saw a great multitude; and He was moved with compassion for them."

Instead of being frustrated and irritated that they weren't giving Him some privacy, Jesus instead had compassion on that enormous crowd!

That kind of love does not come naturally to any of us. Yet, it's the type of love God requires us to have if we are to be His witnesses in this world. First John 4:8 says, "He who does not love does not know God, for God is love."

So how do we get this kind of love? If you need replacement parts for your vehicle, you go to an auto parts shop. If you need groceries you go to the supermarket. Likewise, if we want to grow in our ability to love, we should go to the source of love, which, of course, is God.

"The love of God has been poured out in our hearts by the Holy Spirit who was given to us" (Romans 5:5). Galatians 5:22 says that "the fruit of the Spirit is love." The kind of undeserved love that Christ has for us, and that we are to have for others, is not natural; it is supernatural and therefore, can only come from God.

Day 6—Majority Rule Does Not Equal Right

Years ago, during the housing bubble, a majority of home buyers were in a frenzy to purchase real estate. Sellers would put their homes up for sale one day and by the next they had multiple offers to choose from, many over and above the asking price! Seeing the majority of buyers getting all worked up over purchasing a home just perpetuated the frenzy. The collective impatience of a majority of buyers created an exaggerated "demand" which drove up the price of real estate everywhere. Then the bubble popped and prices fell back to where they should have been all along. Many people ended up with devalued homes and mortgages they couldn't really afford.

Being swayed by the impatience of a "majority" is a dangerous place to be, especially as a Christian. Often, impatience is simply the fruit of unbelief. We must be careful that we do not become impatient with God's timing and that we don't allow ourselves to be affected by the impatience of others.

I love the example that Joshua and Caleb set in scripture of standing firm against the impatience and unbelief of the majority. In Numbers 13, God instructs Moses to send out twelve spies to gather information about the land which God had promised the people of Israel. When the spies returned, ten of them (the majority) gave a bad report of God's promise saying in verse 32 that, "The land through which we have gone as spies is a land that devours its inhabitants." The spies' unbelief spread to the entire congregation of people to the point that they said to Moses in Numbers 14:2-3, "If only we had died in the land of Egypt...Would it not be better for us to return to Egypt?" Because of the spies' unbelief the entire group was willing to go back into bondage!

Yet two of the spies, Joshua and Caleb, had faith in God's promise and perfect timing. Their response in Numbers 14:7-8 is one of faith—"The land we passed through to spy out is an exceedingly good land. If the Lord delights in us, then He will bring us into this land and give it to us, a 'land which flows with milk and honey.'" As a result of their faith, Joshua and Caleb eventually entered the Promised Land, but the unbelieving majority died in the wilderness and never witnessed God's promise fulfilled.

God does not succumb to the will of the majority and neither should we. God alone reigns supreme and if He truly is our "Lord" then we as His followers must obey, whether it fits our timing or not.

Day 7—God Wants to Use You; Yes, YOU!

Have you ever felt that there was no way that God could use someone like you? You may think that people don't ever listen to what you have to say, or maybe you don't have the right background or education, maybe you think you've made too many mistakes, are too young, or perhaps you're just new to being a Christian.

Yet Paul says in First Corinthians 1:26-29:

> For you see your calling, brethren, that not many wise according to the flesh, not many mighty, not many noble, are called. But God has chosen the foolish things of the world to put to shame the wise, and God has chosen the weak things of the world to put to shame the things which are mighty…that no flesh should glory in His presence.

Let me tell you that God specializes in using "unlikely" people to accomplish His purposes. Remember the young boy David, who slew the giant Goliath, and later went on to be King of Israel? Or how about the murderer/outcast Moses who, according to Exodus 4:10, was "slow of speech and slow of tongue" and yet God used him to deliver Israel from slavery in Egypt? How about the self-righteous persecutor of the early Christians, Saul, who later became the same Paul who brought the gospel to the Gentiles? Consider Jesus' very own selection of twelve ordinary everyday men, mostly fishermen, who set the world on fire!

I like Moses' question to God, when God selected him. In Exodus 3:11 Moses says, "Who am I that I should go to Pharaoh, and that I should bring the children of Israel out of Egypt?" Indeed, who are ANY of us to be used by God?

The amazing truth is that God likes to use the foolish to shame the wise and the weak to shame the strong because the glory justly goes to Him, because it belongs to Him! The problem is that when we see ourselves as more than capable, we tend to move forward without Him, or even worse, take the credit for ourselves. Yet God alone deserves the glory.

So what was God's response to Moses? I love it! He said, "Who has made man's mouth? Or who makes the mute, the deaf, the seeing, or the blind? Have not I, the Lord? Now therefore, go, and I will be with your mouth and teach you what you shall say" (Exodus 4:11-12).

So don't worry about your apparent lack of influence, talent, knowledge, age, or your past. If God wants to use you, no shortcoming of yours will stand in His way!

Day 8—Blessed Be the Name of the Lord

At any given point in life we may find ourselves in a season of difficulty or perhaps everything is coming together just as planned. Regardless of where we're at right this moment, I can guarantee that at some point in the near future we will find ourselves in the opposite scenario. That's what the life of an imperfect human being living in an imperfect world is like—some days we are on top of the world and other days it can feel like we are face-down in the mud!

The question is: does our attitude change depending on our circumstances or does it remain constant? In the book of Job, we see how in one day he lost his children and his possessions. Yet how did he react? Job 1:21 documents his response—"The Lord gave, and the Lord has taken away; blessed be the name of the Lord."

It's easy to praise God when He gives and much harder when He takes. Yet, if we only praise God when we feel our lives are going well, how are we any different from those in the world? Even people who aren't Christians thank God when things go well for them! A true test of our faith is when God takes away and we *still* praise Him.

Today, let's consider how we respond toward God in good times and in bad. Do we praise Him only when we are satisfied with life's outcomes (like when we land a big job promotion or receive an unexpected check in the mail), but curse Him when our plans fall apart? Or like Job, do we give God the glory even in the bad times, knowing that He is using those tough times to make us more like Jesus?

Besides, if we are truly honest with ourselves, I think we will find that although God in His sovereignty does both giving and taking, it seems in His love and generosity He always gives much more than He ever takes!

Day 9—Bitterness Leaves a Bitter Taste

I remember when I was a child I had a book of children's science experiments that could be done at home. One of the experiments was to take a small plant, roots and all, and to place it in a cup of water where the water had been dyed with red food coloring. The roots would suck up the colored water and you could see the red dye in the veins of the plant. The experiment showed how the roots work to bring nourishment to the plant. However, the roots can also work against the plant by spreading poison.

The author of Hebrews speaks of the "root of bitterness" in chapter 12 verse 15. Bitterness is indeed a poison that will sour the life of the person who lays claim to it. Ironically, it isn't the person who the bitterness is aimed at that suffers, but the person who refuses to let the bitterness go. Like the red dye in the plant, bitterness will spread its poison throughout your life and soon you will be in bondage to it. In Acts 8:23, Peter confronted a man named Simon with the following words—"For I see that you are poisoned by bitterness and bound by iniquity."

How accurately those words describe the Jewish leaders in Acts 25, who even after Paul was imprisoned for two years, were still seeking to bring false accusations and death against him. Only bitterness could keep a grudge going that long…and Paul hadn't even done anything wrong!

Bitterness leads to hatred, revenge, and even death—the death of joy and relationships. It can even lead to diminished physical and mental health, or cause a person to make dangerous decisions that may put their very life at risk. Job 21:25 says a "man dies in the bitterness of his soul." That is Satan's plan, to "steal, and to kill, and to destroy" (John 10:10).

In contrast, Jesus said in the same scripture, "I have come that they may have life, and that they may have it more abundantly." Jesus forgave us and He tells His followers to do the same to others. In fact, Jesus said in Luke 6:37, "Forgive, and you will be forgiven."

When we release our bitterness, the chains of bondage are broken and we are free to experience Life once again. As Paul wrote in Colossians 2:13, "And you, being dead in your trespasses…He has made alive together with Him, having forgiven you all trespasses."

The path of forgiveness brings healing and life. The path of bitterness will just leave us with a bitter taste in our mouth. The choice is ours. I pray we choose life!

Day 10—Promises in the Desert

Oh, that they had such a heart in them that they would fear Me and always keep all My commandments, that it might be well with them and with their children forever! – Deuteronomy 5:29

What a powerful statement from the mouth of God! These words were spoken by God, to Moses, regarding the children of Israel, just as they were preparing to enter the Promised Land that God had given them. Yet these powerful words are just as relevant for us today.

In this simple statement we see the compassionate heart of God. I can only imagine the depth of feeling as He lovingly looks out over His people, and expresses His desire and expectations for them.

So what does God expect from us? In this verse, God states two expectations: He wants us to fear Him and He wants our obedience.

What does the Bible say regarding fearing God? It says in Proverbs 1:7 that "The fear of the Lord is the beginning of knowledge." To be wise we must fear God first. It's the first step toward attaining godly wisdom. And what is godly wisdom? Simply put, it is wisdom that brings us to a deeper knowledge and understanding of who God is and how He works in our lives.

Fearing God does not imply that we are afraid of Him in the sense that we cower under our beds waiting for a sudden lightning strike from heaven. Remember, God loves us; He doesn't want us to be frightened of Him! But He does want our respect and reverence. When we fear God, we are never forgetting that despite how much He cherishes us, He is still the King of Kings and the Lord of Lords, Creator of the universe, and awesome in power and majesty!

Regarding obedience, Jesus said in John 14:15, "If you love Me, keep My commandments." In other words, if we truly love God, we *must* obey Him.

Isn't it interesting that what God expects of us comes with its own rewards? God asks us to fear Him and in return we begin to attain godly wisdom. We get to *know* God in a personal way! And through obedience we show God how much we love Him. So both the fear of God and obedience bring us closer to God by giving us a deeper knowledge of Him and a more intimate loving relationship with Him.

Let's remember that profound truth as we pursue a deeper relationship with God. Our God is a generous God, and He rewards those who diligently and faithfully seek after Him.

Day 11—The Best Dad Ever

No parent is perfect. All of us are just human beings, saved by grace, and doing our best to raise children in this fallen world. If you're a parent you've probably already discovered that being a parent is not as easy as it seems.

That being said, there are most certainly parents that are extremely poor examples for their kids. One thing I have learned as a dad is that my words can lift up my children or tear them down. Through my actions, I can send the message that they are precious to me or that other things are more important than them.

A parent has the power to seriously impact the life of a child. With great power comes great responsibility, but some parents in this world don't realize the profound impact their actions have on their children.

I don't know your unique situation, but if you come from a home where unconditional love and support weren't part of the daily experience, or if you come from a home impacted by divorce, I have some encouraging words for you.

Psalm 27:10 states, "When my father and my mother forsake me, then the Lord will take care of me."

The Hebrew word for "forsake" in the above verse can also be translated "to leave, abandon, or neglect." Sadly, too many children in this world can relate to being forsaken by a parent. It's totally possible for parents to emotionally abandon a child without even having to leave the home.

The good news is that we have a Heavenly Father who will take care of us and will never let us down. Jesus Christ will never leave us or abandon us.

The idea behind the phrase "take care of me" is that God will take in, receive, or gather us to Himself. In other words, we are a priceless, precious creation to our Father in heaven. He always wants to spend time with us and He is never too busy.

One of my favorite promises that Jesus made, one that brings me constant hope and joy, is in Matthew 28:20 when Jesus said, "I am with you always, even to the end of the age." That means Jesus is never going to leave us.

I want to encourage you to always remember whether your relationship with your earthly parents is a positive one or not, you will always have a perfect Heavenly Father. If you are a child of God, you already have the best Dad ever!

Day 12—Stand By Me

Have you ever wished that someone would stand by you no matter what the circumstance? When a man and woman get married, they often share wedding vows that may say something similar to, "I offer you my solemn vow to be your faithful partner in sickness and in health, in good times and in bad, and in joy as well as in sorrow." These simple words express the promise to "stand by" one another. These are words of commitment and faithfulness. When you promise to stand by someone, you are committing yourself to them.

In Acts 27, we read that in the midst of the turbulent storm at sea, while the ship was being tossed violently by the waves, God was still standing by Paul. Verses 23-24 state, "For there stood by me this night an angel of the God to whom I belong and whom I serve, saying, 'Do not be afraid, Paul.'" God was aware of Paul's circumstances and He sent an angel to remind Paul that He was standing by him during the storm. What a beautiful example of God's commitment to us during the violent storms of life.

This should not come as a surprise, but should instead be a reminder to us of the everlasting faithfulness of our Savior. In Joshua 1:5, God states, "I will not leave you nor forsake you." This is why the psalmist declares in Psalm 89:1, "I will sing of the mercies of the Lord forever; with my mouth will I make known Your faithfulness to all generations." Our God is truly faithful. In fact, He is the very definition of faithfulness. People may come and go in our lives, but God never leaves us. He is always standing by us in the good times and bad.

Perhaps like Paul, you are going through one of life's vicious storms right now. You may feel alone and abandoned. Though you may feel that way, nothing could be further from the truth. God promises repeatedly in His Word that in those moments, He is by our side, ready to comfort us. Psalm 18:2 proclaims, "The Lord is my rock and my fortress and my deliverer; my God, my strength, in whom I will trust; my shield and the horn of my salvation, my stronghold."

The enemy wants us to believe that God has turned His back on us, but God wants us to know that He is standing by us, no matter what. As Hebrews 10:23 states, "Let us hold fast the confession of our hope without wavering, for He who promised is faithful." Do you want someone to stand by you no matter what the circumstance? You already have Him. His name is Jesus Christ.

Day 13—God IS Love

For most of us, it is natural to wonder and speculate about what God is like. The Bible is full of information, telling us about the nature of God and one of the most powerful statements comes from First John 4:8 which says, "He who does not love does not know God, for God is love." In other words, God is the creator, the essence, the source of real love. When we love someone in an unselfish way, we are reflecting that part of God that He has placed in all of us. What do I mean by that? Consider a painter and his masterpiece. Is there not an element of the painter *in* his masterpiece? I'm certain the painter would say there is. God created mankind and as His creation, there is a reflection of Him in all of us.

Consider His statement in Genesis 1:26 which says, "Let Us make man in Our image, according to Our likeness." This statement can be a bit confusing because when we think of "likeness" we think in physical terms, but God isn't confined by the physical world because He is spirit. So instead, think of it from a different perspective. Just as children physically resemble their parents, have you also noticed that they can spiritually resemble their parents, too? Ever heard someone say that a child has a short temper like her father or is sensitive to those who are hurting like his mother? We tend to focus on our physical similarities with our parents, but we share similarities in spirit as well.

So when we love someone with godly love, we "resemble" our Heavenly Father and we may not even realize it!

Which leads to the next question: what is unselfish, godly love? Paul wrote in First Corinthians 13:4-8:

> Love suffers long and is kind; love does not envy; love does not parade itself, is not puffed up; does not behave rudely, does not seek its own, is not provoked, thinks no evil; does not rejoice in iniquity, but rejoices in the truth; bears all things, believes all things, hopes all things, endures all things. Love never fails.

If you truly have a heart to understand who God is and what He is like, go back and read those verses again, only this time substitute the name "Jesus" in place of the word "love." If you do, I think you will get a much clearer picture of what God is like and what He has called us to be if we are truly His children. That is why John wrote, "He who does not love does not know God" because when we know God, and I mean truly know Him, we will resemble His likeness more and more.

Day 14—Whiter Than Snow

Some time back I had the awesome opportunity to be up in the mountains while it was snowing. It was gorgeous to see a fresh blanket of snow covering all the buildings and trees. Everything looked new and clean. There could have been trash on the ground and you wouldn't have known it because the snow covered everything up.

It reminded me of Isaiah 1:18 which states, "Though your sins are like scarlet, they shall be as white as snow." Another scripture that compares God's cleansing of our sins to the whitening of snow is Psalm 51:7 which says, "Wash me, and I shall be whiter than snow."

Have you eaten fresh snow before? A few years ago, I was at a winter retreat in the mountains and the snow didn't let up for two entire days. At one point, I was outside and the snow was up to my knees. It looked so pure and appealing, and even though I haven't done it since I was a little kid, I couldn't help myself from scooping up a handful and eating it.

Now, if the snow had been dirty, like the snow on the side of the road after the snowplows have mixed it with dirt and gravel, I wouldn't even have picked it up with my hands much less eaten it. But pure, untainted snow—I just couldn't help myself!

In our natural state, in our sin, we are gross and disgusting, but when Jesus comes into our lives He cleanses us and makes our lives look like pure, untainted snow! It is the mighty work of His love and grace upon the cross that allows us to be cleansed in this way. First John 1:7 says the "blood of Jesus Christ His Son cleanses us from all sin." Revelation 1:5 tells us that He "loved us and washed us from our sins in His own blood."

Isn't it amazing that it was the crimson red of Jesus' blood that washes us and miraculously makes us white as snow? When we are washed by His blood, all our sinful ugliness is replaced by His beauty. All our wretchedness is removed and He sees us clothed in the very purity of His own blood that He has washed us in.

That's why David proclaimed in Psalm 51:2, "Wash me thoroughly from my iniquity, and cleanse me from my sin." Only the grace of God can do that kind of deep cleaning in our lives. Do you need cleansing? Turn to Jesus for "though your sins are like scarlet, they shall be as white as snow."

Just like every time we see a rainbow we probably think of God's promise to Noah, I hope every time we see snow, we are reminded of the redemptive power of the cross.

Day 15—Flattery Isn't Flattering

If I were to challenge you to quickly give me a list of biblical sins, would you include flattery? When we think of the many different kinds of sin noted in scripture we often overlook the sin of flattery. Yet flattery is indeed a sin. Why? Because at the heart of flattery is both deceitfulness and manipulation.

Proverbs 29:5 warns, "A man who flatters his neighbor spreads a net for his feet." What kind of net? The kind of net you use to trap something. Beware of someone who flatters because they are laying a trap for you. They can't be trusted.

Consider also that flattery is a character trait of the wicked. Psalm 5:9 describes, "For there is no faithfulness in their mouth; their inward part is destruction; their throat is an open tomb; they flatter with their tongue." Ouch! That is not how I would want to be described.

Instead, our speech should reflect the work of Jesus Christ in our lives. As Paul wrote in Ephesians 4:15, we, "speaking the truth in love, may grow up in all things into Him who is the head—Christ." In other words, a mature believer is one who speaks words of truth and love.

Finally, Ephesians 4:29 states, "Let no corrupt word proceed out of your mouth, but what is good for necessary edification, that it may impart grace to the hearers." A follower of Jesus speaks words that edify (build up) those who hear; a flatterer lays a trap to destroy the person who is listening. As Christians, flattery should have no place in our lives.

I suppose that means flattery isn't very flattering for the person who does it!

Day 16—The Power of Unusual Kindness

I remember when I was a youth, I had a season of rebellion against the Lord. By the time I was a freshman in high school, I wrongly blamed God for my problems and felt abandoned by Him, so I attempted to live my life on my own terms, which only led me further into darkness. Then the Lord sent me a godly group of true friends at just the right time, who showed me "unusual kindness" and in doing so, shined the love and light of Jesus Christ into my life. When I saw agape love flowing through average kids just like me, it rekindled a hunger in me to return to the Lord who loves me completely. Such is the power of unusual kindness.

In Acts 28:2, after Paul was shipwrecked on the island of Malta, Luke writes, "And the natives showed us unusual kindness; for they kindled a fire and made us all welcome, because of the rain that was falling and because of the cold." God used the unusual kindness of the inhabitants of Malta to bless Paul and to meet his needs, but whether they realized it or not, it was really God showing His love and provision for Paul through them.

In the same way, we are to be conduits for God's love to the people around us. Why? Because as Second Corinthians 5:14 states, "For the love of

Christ compels us." Jesus poured out His mercy and grace upon us, and love is the supernatural byproduct. First John 4:11 says, "Beloved, if God so loved us, we also ought to love one another."

Jesus set the ultimate example of demonstrating for us what it means to show unusual kindness. Jesus said it clearly in John 15:12 for all of us to follow, "This is My commandment, that you love one another as I have loved you." And how exactly does He love us? Verse 13 says, "Greater love has no one than this, than to lay down one's life for his friends." That's how.

I am a living testimony of the power of the love of Jesus Christ manifested through one person to another. The power of unusual kindness demonstrating the love of Christ to another person is available to each one of us because the Holy Spirit dwells within us. As those who are loved by Christ and have received His grace and mercy, we have the privilege and responsibility of shining that love out to the world around us! In doing so, we will have the profound joy of knowing that we are being used as instruments of God.

Day 17—A Bondservant First

Imagine you are a witness to the last meal that Jesus shared with His disciples the night of His betrayal. Not long before, multitudes were praising Him shouting "Hosanna!" The disciples must have felt a surge of adrenaline. The kingdom of heaven must have certainly felt closer than it ever had before with Christ's triumphal entry into Jerusalem. Suddenly, Jesus stands up from supper, picks up a towel, pours water into a basin, and begins to wash their feet. Can you imagine the look of shock on the disciples' faces when Jesus, their Lord, stoops down to wash and dry their dirty feet?

Paul wrote in Philippians 2:5-7:

> Let this mind be in you which was also in Christ Jesus, who, being in the form of God, did not consider it robbery to be equal with God, but made Himself of no reputation, taking the form of a bondservant, and coming in the likeness of men.

The Greek word for "bondservant" was *doulos* which meant a slave, the lowest status on the social ladder, but not just any slave—a slave by *choice*. The word describes someone who was willingly subject to his master. Paul goes on to write in verse 8, "And being found in appearance as a man, He humbled

Himself and became obedient to the point of death, even the death of the cross." In other words, Jesus humbled Himself and obediently subjected Himself to the will of the Father, so that we in our wretched sinfulness could be saved.

Paul tells us that our mindset should be just like Christ's. He is the example we are to follow! Jesus laid out that example in Matthew 20:27-28 when He stated, "And whoever desires to be first among you, let him be your slave—just as the Son of Man did not come to be served, but to serve, and to give His life a ransom for many." Again, the same word for "slave" in Matthew 20:27 is the same word Paul used to describe Christ as a bondservant in Philippians 2:7, which is *doulos*. This is the example Jesus set for His followers.

In Romans 1:1, Paul then refers to himself as, "a bondservant [*doulos*] of Jesus Christ, called to be an apostle, separated to the gospel of God." Paul understood the example that his Lord had laid before him. Paul knew that he was first and foremost a slave to Christ, then after that an apostle called by God. He had his priorities straight because he knew exactly who was Lord of his life.

Is Jesus your Lord? Then follow His example and serve Him by serving one another with humility and love.

Day 18—The Greatest Sign and Wonder

In my early twenties, a friend of mine who is a pastor invited me to his church to visit. He wanted me to be present to listen to a guest speaker who was gifted in prophecy. This speaker held himself to a high level of accountability, even going so far as to record what the Lord gave him to say and then giving the recording to each person he prayed over.

I still remember what he prayed over me, even though decades have passed since that moment. I know for a fact that he prayed prophetically because everything that he told me would happen has indeed come true. He was authentically gifted and the fruit that followed proved it. Yet, even this experience pales in comparison to something greater!

Paul knew the fruit that followed his ministry authenticated his calling as an apostle. In Second Corinthians 12:12, Paul writes, "Truly the signs of an apostle were accomplished among you with all perseverance, in signs and wonders and mighty deeds." There was some serious fruit that followed Paul's ministry: lives were being changed for the kingdom, people were repenting of their sin and following the Lord, and people were hungry for the Word of God and the will of God. Of course, Paul was used by the Lord to perform amazing miracles as well, but miracles don't necessarily mean someone's heart has been changed. The most powerful sign and wonder of Paul's calling was the very church he was writing to!

Let's pray every day that God will use us in a mighty way to perform signs and wonders in people's lives. Let's pray that God will use us as instruments in His hands to bring people to salvation. There are numerous signs and wonders that God can work through our lives, but I want to see the fruit of the greatest sign and wonder of all—lives that have been permanently transformed and changed by Jesus! How about you?

Day 19—Battle of the Bands

When I was in high school, thanks to a godly mentor in my life, I began to play guitar and lead worship. For a season, I even led a worship band for our weekly chapel services. I wasn't the only one though—there was a second worship band that was much edgier. It's embarrassing to admit, but looking back there was actually a rivalry between the two worship bands. The other band considered themselves more relevant and we considered ourselves more worshipful. We were both vying for the same platform, while at the same time trying to keep the other band off it! Unfortunately, I allowed my flesh to get the victory on several occasions. Looking back, instead of fighting we should have been unified by the common purpose of bringing attention to God, not ourselves. The truth is God had gifted both bands differently in order to minister to a different audience. Too bad we never got passed ourselves to see the incredible opportunity God had laid out before us.

Unlike the "battle of the bands," Peter and Paul understood that there was clarity in recognizing each other's gifting in ministry. In doing so, all the bases were covered and both the Jews and the Gentiles were ministered to and blessed. As Paul wrote in Galatians 2:7-8:

The gospel for the uncircumcised had been committed to me, as the gospel for the circumcised was to Peter (for He who worked effectively in Peter for the apostleship to the circumcised also worked effectively in me toward the Gentiles).

Peter affirmed Paul's gifting to the Gentiles and Paul affirmed Peter's gifting to the Jews. It wasn't a competition, it was just a matter of recognizing and encouraging each other's strengths. The result was the greater plan that God was working in and through them was accomplished!

Today, let us purpose in our hearts to affirm and encourage the gifts each of us have in Christ. Life is not meant to be a carnal competition between spiritual siblings. We all serve a unique role in the body of Christ, so let's not undermine, discourage, or attack each other. Let's not be jealous of one another's gifts and ministries, as if we're adversaries playing on opposing teams. Our enemy wants to divide and conquer us, but may we never allow him the satisfaction. When we work together as a team we complement each other and God will use us to accomplish greater works for His glory. God wants to do a mighty work in and through each one of us today, so let's cheer each other on, not tear each other down.

Day 20—Separate, Not Absent

Years ago, when Juanita and I were still newlyweds, she had a job working for a family-run packaging company. As a Christian, she struggled with the environment of that job because the owners were very carnal and brought witchcraft into the workplace. Juanita wanted to leave so badly that over a period of several months she responded to fifty job postings, but never once received so much as an acknowledgement of her applications. Eventually, we both came to the conclusion that though we couldn't understand why, God clearly wanted her to stay at that job.

In Matthew 5:13-14, Jesus calls us "salt" and "light." Salt and light profoundly affect the environment they are in. Salt enhances the flavor of food (food does not enhance the flavor of salt) and light repels the darkness (darkness does not repel the light). As Christians, we are called to influence the world around us, while not being influenced by the world ourselves. This is how we exist in the world while remaining separate from it. Jesus called us out of the world, yet He also said, "Go therefore and make disciples of all the nations" (Matthew 28:19).

Our separation is not meant to keep us hidden. It's hard to ignore the presence of salt and light, and it should be even more difficult to ignore the presence of the church of God. In other words, our presence should be noticeable and it should be felt by the world around us.

A few weeks after Juanita gave up her job search, she invited one of her coworkers to come to church with us the following Sunday. That morning, both her coworker and her husband became believers. The next Sunday, they brought their daughters who also accepted Jesus Christ as their Lord and Savior. The following week the aunts and uncles came forward. This continued for weeks after, as an incredible harvest took place in the lives of that family, and Juanita was privileged to be a part of it.

Not long after, we noticed a job posting for a local Christian camp. Without any striving or stress, Juanita applied for that one job—and she was hired! It all happened in God's perfect timing.

You see, we are called to be set apart from the world, but we are also called to influence it by shining the light of Jesus Christ so bright that they are blinded by it. This fallen world can be a dark and ugly place, and as children of God we often feel uncomfortable and awkward in it. That's because we don't belong here—our citizenship is in heaven! Yet, for such a time as this, we are here and we have a purpose to fulfill for our Lord's glory. We are called to be separate, not absent, so let's go out and impact this world for Jesus Christ!

Day 21—Jesus, the Origin of the Gospel

For by Him all things were created that are in heaven and that are on earth, visible and invisible...All things were created through Him and for Him. – Colossians 1:16

I often look around at the world and marvel at all the beauty that God has made. John 1:3-4 says, "All things were made through Him, and without Him nothing was made that was made. In Him was life, and the life was the light of men." James 1:17 states, "Every good gift and every perfect gift is from above, and comes down from the Father of lights, with whom there is no variation or shadow of turning." Everything good and beautiful originates in God. Everything.

The gospel (translated "good tidings" from Greek), the good news by which the salvation of mankind is revealed, also has its origin in God. Paul wrote in Romans 1:16, "For I am not ashamed of the gospel of Christ." The good news itself is all about Christ and therefore, originates from Christ Himself.

What exactly is the gospel and why is it good news? Paul wrote in First Corinthians 15:1, 3-4, "Moreover, brethren, I declare to you the gospel...that Christ died for our sins according to the Scriptures, and that He was buried, and that He rose again the third day according to the Scriptures." The gospel is all about what Christ did to allow for the salvation and redemption of mankind. In other words, there is no true gospel apart from Jesus Christ!

Paul goes on to write in First Corinthians 15:21-22, "For since by man came death, by Man also came the resurrection of the dead. For as in Adam all die, even so in Christ all shall be made alive." That truly qualifies as good news! Apart from Christ's finished work on the cross and subsequent resurrection, we were all naturally dead in our sin and on a path to eternal separation from God (Romans 6:23). Yet because of the price He paid, just as He resurrected from the dead, so we can be resurrected from the death brought on by sin and made alive again in Christ, to spend eternity in fellowship with Him!

Of all the beautiful creations that God has made, the gospel is probably the most beautiful one of all! It truly is, as Romans 1:16 proclaims, "the power of God to salvation for everyone who believes."

Day 22—When the Fog Falls

The other day, on the way to church, there was a heavy fog when I left my home. I literally couldn't see more than thirty feet in any direction. The fog was so thick as I was coming up the road that I had my windshield wipers on full blast and both side windows were down in an attempt to help me gain some additional visibility. At one point, I realized I was drifting a little too close to the curb and later a parked car on the side of the street seemed to materialize out of nowhere.

I found myself driving much more carefully, I slowed down well below the speed limit, and I was far less self-assured in my driving skills. I've been driving for decades and yet driving in a deep fog actually reminded me of what it felt like to be a brand new driver—it felt humbling.

Paul knew what it felt like to have the right pedigree and credentials. He knew what it felt like to have such an intimate walk with the Lord that he had the privilege of receiving the gospel from Jesus Christ and to even be shown a glimpse of heaven! The flesh in any mortal man might swell with confidence in such revelations and impressive background. So Paul tells us in Second Corinthians 12:7, "And lest I should be exalted above measure by the abundance of the revelations, a thorn in the flesh was given to me, a messenger of Satan to buffet me, lest I be exalted above measure."

Have you ever been buffeted? Imagine someone striking you with their fist—it's humbling to say the least. Paul's thorn in the flesh was designed to remind him of his dependence on God and not on himself. In other words, his weakness was meant to keep him humble.

Sometimes, we can have a difficult time accepting that God knows what is best for us. As Christians, we have no problem agreeing with that truth intellectually, but when it comes to accepting specific circumstances, we struggle. Why did I lose my job? Why did my spouse leave me? Why am I sick? These are all genuine, heartfelt questions and I believe God is gracious with us when we ask, but what we sometimes forget in our specific circumstance is that He is teaching us something.

Today, when the fog falls, let's embrace God's ways of keeping us humbly dependent on Him. It may not always be easy, but we must stand on the truth that our Heavenly Father knows what is best for us.

Day 23—Mesmerized Mayhem

When my children were little, I assembled a wood swing set with a clubhouse for them to enjoy. Everything was going well until I reached a point in the assembly where I needed to balance a long wood beam so that I could secure it to the frame on both ends. The problem was I needed to hold up one end while I bolted the other side. It was a two-person job (as the instructions clearly stated), but I was home alone. So I came up with the clever idea to use a ladder to support the beam in the middle. After securing the beam on both ends, I then began to lay the floor panels for the upper story of the clubhouse across the long wood beam.

I was mesmerized in the project, totally "in the zone," and so fascinated by the process that it didn't hit me until I bumped up against the ladder that I had foolishly run the beam through the ladder, then placed the floor panels, so that the ladder was literally built *inside* the swing set! I was so frustrated that for a few minutes I even contemplated sawing the ladder in pieces to get it out! In the end, I had to disassemble the entire floor just to remove my ladder.

Likewise, the churches of Galatia had become mesmerized, fascinated by false teaching, so that they too were in danger of losing their way. Paul writes in Galatians 3:1, "O foolish Galatians! Who has bewitched you that you should not obey the truth, before whose eyes Jesus Christ was clearly portrayed among you as crucified?" The Galatians were being led away from the truth because they were becoming mesmerized by a lie. They were so fascinated by the false teaching of the Judaizers that Paul likened them to being "bewitched." In the figurative sense, it was as if someone had placed a spell on them. This fascination was causing them to stray from the truth of Christ's completed work on the cross.

Let's guard ourselves from those things that might distract us by occupying our hearts and minds away from Jesus Christ. Our flesh is easily susceptible to being bewitched by the empty facades this world offers us. In fact, our flesh craves to be mesmerized by the things of this world. Instead, I pray that we would all walk in the Spirit, with eyes fixed on Jesus, so that He and He alone would capture our fascination and attention.

Like my ladder which was foolishly built into the swing set because I was focused on the wrong thing, to be mesmerized by anything other than Jesus will only bring mayhem into your life!

Day 24—God Revealed

Ever since I was a little boy, I have often found peace and perspective from life's trials by viewing God's power and majesty through His creation. When I pause to admire creation, I can clearly see and feel the presence of God. It reminds me of how an artist, while expressing himself in a painting, leaves clues and traces of who he is in the masterpiece. The universe is God's canvas and creation is His masterpiece. The late painter, Thomas Kinkade, literally had a small strand of his hair imbedded in his signature on his paintings as proof that the painting was authentic. The essence of the creator is always evident in the creation. This is how God reveals Himself through the material world around us.

Romans 1:20 says, "For since the creation of the world His invisible attributes are clearly seen, being understood by the things that are made, even His eternal power and Godhead, so that they are without excuse." Thomas Kinkade had a very unique style that has often been imitated, but never replicated. His influence in other artists' work is evident, but there is always something slightly off. A true Kinkade painting can usually be spotted a mile away. God makes it even less confusing for mankind because His style can neither be imitated nor replicated!

The Greek word for "without excuse" is *anapologetos* and it literally means "that which cannot be defended" or is "inexcusable." Paul is telling us that it is inexcusable for someone not to see the attributes of God, such as His divine nature, in creation. Just like a true Kinkade painting can be spotted from a distance, Paul is saying that God's divinity is blatantly obvious in the material world He spoke into existence. This is why David wrote in Psalm 14:1, "The fool has said in his heart, 'There is no God.'"

You may not be rejecting the existence of God, but are you denying His power to satisfy your needs? Tonight, look up at the stars in the sky and marvel at the vastness of even the small sliver of the universe that you can see from your vantage point. Job 37:14 exhorts us, "Stand still and consider the wondrous works of God." In other words, let's pause from our worries and let's look around at what God has done!

Instead of looking inward at our problems, let's look up! See how God has revealed Himself in the stars, the ocean, and the mountains. The very Creator Himself dwells within you, loves you, and wants to provide for your needs. Looking at how God has revealed Himself in creation is a wonderful reminder of how small our problems are compared to our very big God!

Day 25—Our Motivations Exposed!

I have always found it humorous when Hollywood pokes fun at itself in the classic actor's question, "What's my motivation?" Supposedly, the actor understanding the character's "motivation" will help them do a better job of portraying the character. In real life, no one truly knows the actual motivation of other people because we can only look at their words and actions. We can't truly know what takes place in their heart. There is a great quote which says, "You can fool all the people some of the time, and some of the people all the time, but you cannot fool all the people all the time." In God's case, you can't fool Him ever!

What is in *your* heart? Whatever it may be, God knows, and you can know too! God's Word can reveal to us exactly what "our" motivation is. We can have other people fooled, and sometimes we can even have ourselves fooled, but there is no fooling God. Hebrews 4:12 clearly states, "For the word of God is living and powerful, and sharper than any two-edged sword…and is a discerner of the thoughts and intents of the heart." The Greek word for "discerner" is *kritikos* which means "skilled in judging." In other words, God's Word is a pro and there is no fooling Him.

Hebrews 4:13 continues on to say, "And there is no creature hidden from His sight, but all things are naked and open to the eyes of Him to whom we must give account." This is the reason why God said in First Samuel 16:7, "For the Lord does not see as man sees; for man looks at the outward appearance, but the Lord looks at the heart."

This should be a sobering realization that there are no secrets that you can keep from God. Just like Jonah learned, there is nowhere we can run or hide from the Lord. Yet amazing joy should also follow this truth too! We often fear people truly knowing us because we sense they would not love us anymore if they knew how wretched we really are. What a joyful freedom it is to know that the God who created us and knows us intimately, still loves and desires us, despite our flaws and imperfections!

There is freedom in having our motivations exposed! God's Word and the Holy Spirit will reveal our impure motivations, and we need only to confess and repent of those impurities (1 John 1:9). Then we can be free from past guilt and sorrow, so we can move joyfully forward in our intimate relationship with the living God! As Nehemiah 8:10 says, "Do not sorrow, for the joy of the Lord is your strength."

Day 26—Up, Up and Away!

Ever since I can remember, I have always been fascinated by aviation. Even now, a low-flying plane will usually stop me in my tracks. However, in a twist of irony, I don't particularly like flying. In fact, for many years I was actually afraid of flying. In my early twenties, I remember flying from Dallas to Topeka in a small plane that actually had a propeller. I didn't even know commercial planes with propellers still existed! Actually, it was more like a kite with seats. Anyway, halfway to Topeka the plane suddenly just fell from the sky! Everybody on the plane—all nine of us—screamed as if we were going to die. Then, just as suddenly as the plane fell, it caught air again and continued on to our destination. Everybody looked sheepishly around at one another and then burst out laughing.

Fear of death is certainly not uncommon. In fact, a modest dose of it can keep us away from dangerous situations (which is the reason why I'll never go skydiving)! Yet, apart from Jesus Christ, the fear of death, even death itself, holds people in bondage. The author of Hebrews wrote:

> Inasmuch then as the children have partaken of flesh and blood, He Himself likewise shared in the same, that through death He might destroy him who had the

power of death, that is, the devil, and release those who through fear of death were all their lifetime subject to bondage. (Hebrews 2:14-15)

Without Jesus, death, and the subsequent fear associated with it, is bondage, but the resurrection of Christ has released those who believe in Him from the bondage of both fear and death.

As Christians, we have no legitimate cause to fear death. To those without Jesus, death seems to be the end of the road, but as children of God, death is only the gateway from this reality to heaven. Therefore, we have no reason to be afraid of dying. Just as the grave could not contain Christ, even so, the grave will neither contain us. As Paul said, "We are confident, yes, well pleased rather to be absent from the body and to be present with the Lord" (2 Corinthians 5:8).

Christ conquered death by resurrecting from the grave. His victory is ours as well, for we can now rise above the bondage of death because of the One who rose from the dead. For us, death is not the end; it is only the beginning. Our last moment here on this earth will be followed by the next one in the presence of God. This is why we can say, "'Death is swallowed up in victory.' 'O Death, where is your sting? O Hades, where is your victory?'" (1 Corinthians 15:54-55).

Day 27—Don't Pick the Lock

Imagine nearly being arrested on your honeymoon! Juanita and I were honeymooning in Lake Tahoe when I learned the Nevada State Capitol was nearby. In California you can take a tour of the State Capitol and Governor's Mansion, so I added Nevada's to our sightseeing list. After getting directions from an employee at Carl's Jr., we excitedly headed to the Governor's Mansion.

When we parked I thought it was strange that no vehicles were there except for a bunch of black SUVs with tinted windows and huge antennas. Oh well! Blinded by wedded bliss, I confidently walked up to the front door and pulled on the handle—it was locked. "Why is it locked?" I said to Juanita. "The guy at Carl's Jr. told us it would be open." So I attempted to enthusiastically shake the handle loose.

Suddenly, armed men in black uniforms and sunglasses appeared out of nowhere, demanding to know what I was doing. "We're here for the tour," I whimpered from a fetal position on the floor. "There are no tours here," barked the security officer. "This is a private residence and the Governor and his wife are home!" Oops.

In Revelation 3:7 we read, "And to the angel of the church in Philadelphia write, 'These things says He who is holy, He who is true, "He who has the key of David, He who opens and no one shuts, and shuts and no one opens."'" As we look at the church of Philadelphia, a church that serves as a model for us in the last days, we see that Jesus is the One who opens and closes doors in our lives. He who is holy and true has the key of David—some doors He opens and other doors He shuts.

Do we trust His judgment and authority? Do we believe that as our Lord, He has the keys to open and shut the doors in our lives? Today, don't fret over a door that God has closed, don't get upset or flesh out; instead, trust His better judgment and try a different door. In other words, don't try to pick the lock on a door that our Savior has shut; don't jiggle the handle or try to force your way in. If the door is closed, it's closed for a reason.

Believe me, at the end of the day we don't want to be where God doesn't want us to be. If the door is closed, leave it that way and praise Him for His providence. After all, you don't know what might be waiting on the other side—it could be the Governor's security detail!

Day 28—Someone Worth Imitating

Long before I became a parent, I often thought of what it would be like to *be* a parent. Well, now that I have been a Daddy for many years, I know that being a parent is one of the greatest joys in life. One of those joys is to witness your children imitating you.

When he was a little boy, my son, Maksim, especially loved to imitate me. In my closet, where I hang my ties, he used to hang his little "clip on" tie on top. In the drawer where I roll up my belts there used to be another belt that was a fraction of the size of the others. And my cologne bottles used to empty at an increasingly faster rate! When I cut my nails, he wanted to cut his nails. When I worked in the yard, he wanted to work in the yard, too. And when I opened my Bible, he would run to grab his Bible so he could "read" along with me. It truly was a lot of fun to have my "little man" wanting to be like his Daddy, but I was also reminded that it isn't just about fun and games—being a parent is an awesome responsibility and stewardship from the Lord.

Paul tells us in First Corinthians 11:1, "Imitate me, just as I also imitate Christ." The Christian home needs to be a place where parents can say with credibility, "If you look into my life, you will see that I follow Jesus." Of course, this does not mean that a Christian home is perfect—none of our homes are perfect—but a Christian home should be a place where our children can see and know that we are committed to following the Lord.

Here's the thing about kids—they're going to imitate someone. Whether they imitate Iron Man, the firefighter who lives next door, the kids at the skate park who can do cool tricks, or their parents who live out their faith with boldness, deep down inside all children are looking to imitate somebody. One way or the other, that platform will be granted to someone who will speak into their lives, and that person will be an example they imitate. As Christian parents, the question we need to ask is who will fill that role in our children's lives?

God, in His sovereignty, has given us first dibs on that platform. So what will we demonstrate to our kids? Proverbs 22:6 instructs us, "Train up a child in the way he should go, and when he is old he will not depart from it." With the precious, limited time we have, who will we teach them to imitate? Whether our children are infants or adults, it's never too late to begin anew and nothing is impossible for the Lord. Today, let's purpose in our hearts to give our children and our spouse someone worthwhile to imitate in us—let's give them Jesus!

Day 29—Garbage In, Garbage Out

I remember my freshman year of high school I picked up a secular book that was very dark in content. Not long after beginning the book, I began to sense that the days seemed to be gloomy and dark, too. I wasn't feeling like myself either. I was moody, out of sorts, and depressed. This went on steadily for two whole weeks. I kept trying to figure out what was different in my life, when it finally struck me that the nature of the book was affecting my perception of the world around me. I didn't bother finishing the book; instead, I threw it in the trash. I literally felt better after that!

There is an old computer programming term that states, "garbage in, garbage out." The phrase refers to the correlation between bad input data resulting in bad output data. In other words, if you program junk into the computer, the computer will just kick out junk as well. When you think about it, the same is true of the human mind.

As followers of Jesus Christ, who have been bought with the price of His precious blood, we need to ask ourselves, what kinds of things are influencing our perspective? Are our minds fully submitted to Christ? In Philippians 4:8, Paul writes:

> Finally, brethren, whatever things are true, whatever things are noble,

whatever things are just, whatever things are pure, whatever things are lovely, whatever things are of good report, if there is any virtue and if there is anything praiseworthy—meditate on these things.

In contrast, if you turn the above list to its opposite (whatever things are untrue, impure...etc.), we see exactly what we are *not* to allow our minds to meditate or dwell on. Paul's exhortation should be the test by which we weigh the various interests that compete for the attention of our minds.

In Romans 12:2, Paul writes, "And do not be conformed to this world, but be transformed by the renewing of your mind." Have you ever wondered how we are to renew our minds? Let's begin with what we put into our minds. After all, the things which are planted into our minds are what manifest themselves in our actions. Galatians 6:8 states, "For he who sows to his flesh will of the flesh reap corruption, but he who sows to the Spirit will of the Spirit reap everlasting life."

Jesus wants His bride, the church, to be holy and without blemish. So let's think twice about what we look at, what we listen to, and what we do with our bodies, which are the temple of the Holy Spirit. Remember, garbage in, garbage out...good things in, good things out.

Day 30—Nothing Apart from God's Power

A while back I was pulling into the parking lot of Baker's and I noticed a couple across the street trying to push a car that had run out of gas up a steep driveway into a gas station parking lot. No matter how hard they pushed, the car just would not budge—it took everything in them just to keep the car from rolling back into the street! I ran across and gave them a hand. With the extra push, we were able to easily get the car up the driveway.

I was reminded of how everything that we do is based on the power of the Holy Spirit in our lives and apart from Him, we are as powerless as the couple struggling to push their car up the steep driveway. We need God to come alongside us and give us the strength that we lack on our own. Zechariah 4:6 tells us, "'Not by might nor by power, but by My Spirit,' says the Lord of hosts." Our strength is not based in this physical world, but in the spiritual one.

Philippians 4:13 says, "I can do all things through Christ who strengthens me." The implication is clear—*without* Christ we cannot do all things. In fact, in John 15:5, Jesus clearly states, "I am the vine, you are the branches. He who abides in Me, and I in him, bears much fruit; for without Me you can do nothing."

One of the biggest errors we can make as Christians is to fall for the lie that we are capable of doing anything we put our minds to. That is a philosophy of the sinful world we inhabit and it is rooted in pride.

James 4:6 reveals, "God resists the proud, but gives grace to the humble." The Greek word for "resists" is *antitassomai* and it can be translated, "to range in battle against." The picture is that of an army arranging itself in a battle formation, against an opposing force—not exactly a great position to be in against God! Verse 7 goes on to exhort, "Therefore submit to God." The Greek word for "submit" is *hupotasso*, which is also a military term, and this conveys the idea of troops being voluntarily arranged under the command of a leader. Ah, much better!

The truth is that only when we submit to Christ's leadership over our lives, humble ourselves, and make ourselves reliant and utterly dependent on His lordship over us, *then* we will begin to experience the true power of the Holy Spirit in and through our lives.

Day 31—Promise Keeper

Over the years, I have only shared with a handful of people that the Lord promised me when I was fifteen years old that one day I would be in pastoral ministry. Of course, at fifteen that wasn't a promise I necessarily desired Him to make, nor was it expected, but I can still recall the exact moment I heard the Lord's voice. At the time, I wanted to be a movie director, but I remembered the Lord's promise and tucked it away in the back of my mind.

For twenty years I never forgot the Lord's words that He spoke to me that warm summer night in 1990. I never did become a movie director, but I graduated from college, worked my way up the corporate ladder, ran for public office, and started my own business. Though it appeared I was moving further and further away from full-time pastoral ministry, I knew in my soul that one day God would hold true to His promise.

In Matthew 21:2, we see Jesus Christ fulfilling a promise of scripture when He says, "Go into the village opposite you, and immediately you will find a donkey tied, and a colt with her. Loose them and bring them to Me." Jesus performed this action to fulfill the prophecy of Zechariah 9:9, "Behold, your King is coming to you; He is just and having salvation, lowly and riding on a donkey, a colt, the foal of a donkey." This was written 500 years before the Triumphal Entry on Palm Sunday. Why did Jesus do this? Because God always keeps His promises.

Back in 2010, my life took a serious change of direction. It was all part of the story of my life that He had woven for me so long ago. Three years later, what He promised was joyfully fulfilled and so I am gladly reminded of His faithfulness every day of my life. He had always been keeping His promise, working out the details, even when I was blind and couldn't see, even when I forgot or was unfaithful to Him, He was always faithful and true. I didn't see it clearly in the moment, but I see it crystal clear now that I look back in retrospect.

Today, are you wrestling with a promise God has given you? Perhaps you don't see how it could possibly become a reality. Or maybe fear has gripped you that something has changed. Let me encourage you that our God keeps His promises. It may take twenty years, it may take 500 years, but He is always true to His word. Mark my words—the wait will be well worth it!

Day 32—Dying to Live

I was recently reading about a young woman who contracted rare, flesh-eating bacteria after suffering a deep cut on her leg as a result of a zip-lining accident in Georgia. Her initial injury was serious but nowhere near life-threatening, until the necrotizing bacteria went to work. In the end, the woman had to have her left leg, right foot, and both hands amputated in order to save her life. Though doctors tried to save her limbs, eventually they had to cut them off and let them die, in order that she might live.

When I first read about this story it reminded me of the effect of sin in our lives. Sin is like necrotizing bacteria of the soul, eating at a person, killing them along the way. Just like amputating an infected limb, we need to kill the sin before the sin kills us. Eliminating sin from our lives becomes even more urgent when we consider Christ's imminent return.

Romans 13:11-14 says:

> And do this, knowing the time, that now it is high time to awake out of sleep; for now our salvation is nearer than when we first believed. The night is far spent, the day is at hand. Therefore let us cast off the works of darkness, and let us put on the armor of light. Let us walk properly, as in the day, not in revelry and

drunkenness, not in lewdness and lust, not in strife and envy. But put on the Lord Jesus Christ, and make no provision for the flesh, to fulfill its lusts.

We have two choices: we can feed our flesh or we can feed our spirit. The one we feed and nurture will be the stronger of the two. Therefore, knowing sin kills and that our Savior is returning one day soon to take us home, the choice should be obvious. With the countdown clock running out, we need to ensure there is no provision for our flesh to thrive. Instead, we need to starve it out and give it no opportunity to flourish. Let the flesh die by cutting off its food source—sin—and let's put on the righteousness of Jesus Christ instead.

Jesus said it like this, "If anyone desires to come after Me, let him deny himself, and take up his cross daily, and follow Me. For whoever desires to save his life will lose it, but whoever loses his life for My sake will save it" (Luke 9:23-24).

Like weary travelers who hear the whistle of the train in the distance and know their ride will soon round the bend, taking them far away from the station where they patiently wait, prepared to leave at any moment when the train arrives, so let us also be ready. Time is of the essence—our Savior quickly approaches! Let's get busy dying to ourselves, so that we can get busy living for Him!

Day 33—Unadulterated Joy

Some years back, I had to go on a business trip to New York for three weeks. Although it was an incredible experience, it was a struggle for me to be away from my family for such a long period of time. I'll never forget the anticipation of the plane ride home. I remember coming down the escalator at Ontario International Airport with my luggage under one arm and a doll for my daughter, Skylar (who was a toddler at the time), under the other. At the bottom of the escalator, near the baggage claim, I could see my family waiting for me with balloons and smiles.

I will never forget the joy of greeting Skylar as she fell completely into my arms. There were no words to express how good it felt to be home. Sometime later, I saw a photo of the moment Skylar and I greeted each other, seconds before we embraced. The look of pure, unadulterated joy captured on her face brought me to tears—I've never seen anything like it before or since.

As beautiful and perfect as that moment of joy shared with my daughter was, it pales in comparison to the joy that comes as a result of Jesus Christ's finished work on the cross. Apart from the cross, there would be no lasting joy for us because we would still be slaves to sin with a chasm between us and God. Yet because of the cross, we are now free from the bondage and shackles of sin. We are no longer separated from God and we will one day go home to be with Him forever! No other joy can compare to being reunited with our Creator who fashioned and formed us, to be in fellowship with Him—no more separation, no more distance, no more chasm—for eternity! In John 15:11, Jesus says, "These things I have spoken to you, that My joy may remain in you, and that your joy may be full." True joy, complete joy, can only be found in Jesus Christ and the finished work of the cross.

We, as Christians, should be the most joyful people on the planet! Of course, this does not mean we never experience sadness, frustration, or even disappointment, but as believers we should never camp out in those dark places because we have a lasting joy that is a result of our salvation in Christ. This is why Jesus said in John 16:33, "In the world you will have tribulation; but be of good cheer, I have overcome the world."

How did Jesus overcome the world? Christ overcame the world on the cross. Therefore, be of good cheer and be full of unadulterated joy and hope! Thanks to what Jesus accomplished on the cross, our best days, our most joyful days, are still to come!

Day 34—Dead End

The old life, who we were formerly apart from Christ, is a dead end. I learned this the hard way when at nineteen years old, due to a personal, spiritual failure on my part, in shame I returned to the world which I had previously left behind. I can't justify or rationalize what I did, all I can say is it was foolishness on my part to think that after walking intimately with Jesus, I could somehow return to the old life. The result was that I was filled with conflict and sorrow. I no longer belonged to the world; I didn't fit in and I knew I was breaking the heart of my loving Savior who was calling me back home.

In those years of rebellion I suffered needlessly, but eventually, like the Prodigal Son, I came crawling back home and my Heavenly Father took me in with open arms. I can never and will never leave Him again—I am absolutely convinced this world has nothing for me.

Peter, too, had experienced a personal, spiritual failure in his life when he denied Jesus three times on the night of Christ's betrayal. As a result, in shame, he may also have attempted to return to the old life. We read in John 21:2-3:

> Simon Peter, Thomas called the Twin,
> Nathanael of Cana in Galilee, the sons of
> Zebedee, and two others of His disciples

were together. Simon Peter said to them,
"I am going fishing." They said to him,
"We are going with you also." They
went out and immediately got into the
boat, and that night they caught nothing.

Of course, Peter may have had other reasons for
going fishing, but it is still important to note that
fishing had been Peter's life *prior* to following Jesus.
We read in Matthew 4:18-20 that Jesus saw "Peter,
and Andrew his brother, casting a net into the sea; for
they were fishermen. Then He said to them, 'Follow
Me, and I will make you fishers of men.' They
immediately left their nets and followed Him." Peter
left his old life to follow Jesus, but now he was going
fishing; yet, notice the result—he caught nothing.

Today, I believe the Lord wants to remind us that
if we were to attempt to return to our old lives, we,
too, will catch nothing. Are you finding yourself
looking longingly back over your shoulder to the old
life, or perhaps you have already returned there? If
you can relate to this today, please reject and repent
of the old life once and for all. The old life is no
longer who we are because that former version of
ourselves is dead, for we are made alive and new in
Christ. Our old lives are a dead end because this
world truly has nothing for us.

Day 35—Untroubled Heart

Back in 2011, I had to make a big decision: follow the Lord's call to full-time ministry, which meant selling my business, or ignore the Lord's call and maintain the status quo. As a believer, I knew the right decision was to obey my Lord, but as a husband and father, I struggled with questions about how the mortgage would get paid and what we would do if the car broke down or one of us needed to see a doctor.

So I went to the church property to spend time at the cross, seeking the Lord's guidance in prayer. I came to Him with a laundry list of "what if" scenarios and questions. I asked for guarantees and specific timetables. By the time I left, the Lord hadn't given me the answers I wanted; instead, He gave me the answer I needed. "Don't focus on what you don't know…focus on what you *do* know."

Jesus said in John 14:1, "Let not your heart be troubled; you believe in God, believe also in Me." The Greek word for "believe" can also be translated "to trust." In speaking to His disciples, Jesus was essentially saying, "Do you trust Me?" In many ways, this is a question we must answer every day.

When we first come to the cross, we are effectively saying by our commitment to follow Jesus that we trust Him for our eternal salvation, as our Savior. But every day after we must answer the question, do we trust Him as our Lord? Do we trust Him when we are sick, when someone we love walks out on us, when a child goes wayward, when a job comes to an end, or when we're asked to step out in faith into a situation we don't completely understand?

Though our situations are all unique, the answer the Lord gave me that day at the cross really applies to all of us. Life is uncertain and if we camp out on that fact, we, too, will constantly be in a state of uncertainty—that's a troubled heart. Yet, amidst life's uncertainties, there is something we can be completely certain of—we can trust Jesus.

Every day there is a choice we need to make: are we going to focus on life's questions and uncertainties, or are we going to focus on God's promises and assurances? The difference between the two will determine whether we have a troubled heart or an untroubled heart. Let's choose an untroubled heart; let's trust Jesus.

Day 36—God's Delays Are Not Denials

Have you ever had peace about moving a certain direction in life, yet seemingly God kept closing the door? I remember studying for my California Real Estate Exam. Initially, I found myself eligible to take the exam on a whim and entirely just for fun. I did well in the test preparation class, but I spent absolutely zero time preparing for the actual test. I was humbled when I failed it. Believing God was directing me to retake the test, I prepared to meet the challenge a second time. I studied for months. I went in to take the test asking God to either help me pass it, or let me fail it spectacularly so that I would know not to try again. I failed the test by only one question. Unsure how to interpret those results, I took a long break. Eventually, I found myself unexpectedly leaving my job to start my own business—in real estate! Now I desperately *needed* to pass that test to get my license. I broke down and wept when the results of my third attempt revealed that I had finally passed! If I had passed the test the first time I probably wouldn't have cared, but God's timing was perfect (and desperately needed) on round three.

In John's gospel we read the account of Jesus raising His friend, Lazarus, from the dead. When word reached Jesus that Lazarus was very sick, Jesus said, "This sickness is not unto death, but for the glory of God, that the Son of God may be glorified through it" (John 11:4). The phrase "not unto death" meant that death would not be the final outcome of this situation. Jesus was waiting so that He could do an even greater work through Lazarus. It wasn't that Jesus was unconcerned about the death of Lazarus—He loved Lazarus—but He had greater plans to use the death of Lazarus to demonstrate His power over death! You see, healing Lazarus' sickness would have been pretty amazing, but raising him from the dead was downright awesome! God received the greater glory by allowing Lazarus to die.

It's a great reminder for us that God's delays are not denials. He may be asking you to "wait" so that He can do an even bigger miracle in and through your life. Don't be discouraged; don't think that God has abandoned you or checked out of your life. Just like Jesus knew that Lazarus had died, He knows every thought and detail of your life as well…and He loves you! First Peter 5:6-7 tells us, "Therefore humble yourselves under the mighty hand of God, that He may exalt you in due time, casting all your care upon Him, for He cares for you." Always remember that God has a plan for your life. Don't rip yourself off by trying to force His hand or by attempting to get ahead of His plan. Just like Lazarus, we often need to allow our plans to die, so that God can reveal His greater plan for our lives!

Day 37—Keeping it Simple

I find it humorous how we complicate things that are actually quite simple. When I was in my early twenties, as a favor, I drove a friend's mom to a job interview. While she took a written math test, I enjoyed some light conversation with the interviewer. The conversation was so enjoyable that about two hours later we both realized that my friend's mom was *still* taking the test! The test measured basic addition and subtraction, but she was so nervous about impressing him that she had used complex algebraic formulas instead. When he pointed out that she had overcomplicated a simple test, she became upset and walked out of the interview. He was looking for something simple, not complicated. Have you ever confused the two?

It reminds me of how sometimes our fear causes us to overcomplicate sharing the gospel. The gospel isn't complicated, though our enemy wants us to believe it is so that we will be afraid to share it, being deceived into thinking we aren't capable of articulating a complex theological truth. However, it is quite possible for something to be both profound and simple at the same time. The gospel is, as First Corinthians 15:3-4 states, "that Christ died for our sins according to the Scriptures, and that He was buried, and that He rose again the third day according to the Scriptures." And what motivated Jesus Christ to die for our sins? First John 4:9 says, "In this the love of God was manifested toward us, that God has sent His only begotten Son [Jesus Christ] into the world, that we might live through Him." At its core, the gospel is about love.

God, in His divine sovereignty, has chosen us flawed creatures as the vessels to spread His message of love to the lost world around us. Romans 10:17 states, "So then faith comes by hearing, and hearing by the word of God." God's Word is so powerful that it will lead people who hear it to faith. Yet how will people hear God's Word if nobody tells them the message? Jesus said in Matthew 28:19, "Go therefore and make disciples of all the nations, baptizing them in the name of the Father and of the Son and of the Holy Spirit." Jesus gave His disciples a commission, not a suggestion. This isn't a request; no, He is commanding us to do this! And if He truly is our Lord, then we absolutely must obey.

God's motivation is love and it's the love of Christ in us that compels us to share the gospel! Don't allow fear to complicate the simplicity of the good news we have to share with the world. Besides, what is there to fear anyway? If we do as our Lord commands, then we are in His will and there is no safer place to be! Now how simple is that?

Day 38—Setting the Forest on Fire

Do you believe that our words have the power to change lives? There was a time in my life that if someone had posed the same question to me, I would have laughed. I don't deny the power of healing words now though; not since I witnessed the power of words in my own life.

In my adolescence, I thought my future would be meaningless, hopeless, and filled with darkness. Then someone told me that Jesus Christ loves me and though He loves all the billions of people on the planet, I wasn't just a face in the crowd. He loves me and He has a special future planned for us to experience together. Those words cut through the darkness of my heart and made way for His healing light to come flooding in, and the light sparked a fire in my soul. Something was kindled in my heart and it burns to this very day!

James 3:5 tells us, "Even so the tongue is a little member and boasts great things. See how great a forest a little fire kindles!" Fire is an interesting element. It has the power to take life, but it also has the power to sustain life—it just depends on how it's employed. The same is true of our words. With our words we can destroy someone by breaking their spirit, or with our words we can speak life and healing. Our words can do both, it just depends on how we use them.

It doesn't take much to start a forest fire: a thoughtless cigarette thrown out a car window, a careless camper not fully extinguishing the campfire—all it takes is a spark. That's what James is warning us about in the power of the tongue. But what if we used the exact same principle to bring God glory?

If one spark can set a forest ablaze, what if we started a holy fire? What if the spark is our words of life, based on God's Word and His love, and the forest is the hearts of those people who surround us? It wouldn't take much; it's not complicated, it's simple! Just like when I was a teen, if we tell others how much Jesus loves them, how He cherishes them, and desires to spend eternity loving them, what might be ignited in their hearts?

Today, cry out with me for the Holy Spirit to empower us to set the forest of people around us on fire for Jesus Christ! May it be an unquenchable fire that burns mighty and hot, may it spread to others far and wide, and may the effect of its flames be seen for eternity!

Day 39—Who is in Control Now?

At the beginning of summer, I decided that a dietary change was in order. It was time to stop drinking all the soda, eating so much pizza and burgers, and not exercising my body. For two entire months I ate a more balanced diet with lots of fruit and veggies, tons of water, no sweets, and except for the occasional treat, no fast food. I even started exercising!

June was great, but in July I became sicker than I had ever been in my life. In a period of three weeks I had the H1N1 virus, pink eye, and just when I was starting to feel normal again, I caught a cold with a cough that sounded like I was about to keel over at any moment. Then one day I was telling some friends that I've never been bit by a bug above my shoulders and the very next day I woke up with a giant welt on my neck! What was going on? I was doing everything right with regard to my health, but it seemed like everything had been going wrong!

Whenever we go through trials, whether they are great or small, we have a choice whether or not we're going to trust God in the situation. The choice is ours, but God's Word does instruct us on which is the better choice. James 1:6 tells us that whoever prays "let him ask in faith, with no doubting, for he who doubts is like a wave of the sea driven and tossed by the wind." When we face trials, we are to pray without doubting. This demonstrates that we really do believe God is in control of the circumstances of our lives. In fact, trials help us to truly understand that God is in control and we are not. In other words, the circumstance wouldn't be a trial by definition if we could control or stop it at our own choosing, so that proves we're not in control. Once we accept this truth, we can then surrender the situation over to God.

While I was still sick with my cold, I prayed and asked God why I had spent that month sick when I should have been healthy. I was humbled when God reminded me that even though I might take the best possible care of my body the way I should, my health is still ultimately in His hands, not my own. He didn't cause me to be sick, but He allowed it to teach me this valuable lesson. I can't control my health; I can only be a steward of it. God controls my health because He is Lord, not me.

Whatever trials we face today, be reminded that the presence of the trial itself is proof our sense of control is an illusion. We're not in control, but as believers we know who is! Let's trust God who is in control of the entire universe. He can see us through any difficult time...if we don't doubt, but believe!

Day 40—Best Christmas Present Ever!

I love the Christmas season and one of my favorite reasons is giving gifts to my loved ones. Of course, when I was a kid it was receiving gifts that my siblings and I were more interested in!

I remember one Christmas, my brother, Eddie, asked for a remote control airplane. Well, he got one, except it was only remote control in the air. To get it off the ground we had to launch it with a giant rubber band which was connected on one end to the airplane and on the other end to a stake in the ground. It took us hours to assemble the plane and then finally the big moment arrived! We launched the plane successfully into the sky, then my dad turned to Eddie and handed him the remote control. I'll never forget it. Eddie took the remote, made a sudden jerking move with the control stick, and the plane instantly nosedived straight to the ground where it was obliterated in hundreds of pieces!

Hours of assembly and preparation ended in a few short seconds of flight time and a devastating explosion. To this day, I think that was the most short-lived Christmas present I have ever witnessed. The gifts this world has to offer just aren't what they're cracked up to be.

On the other hand, Jesus Christ is our ultimate Christmas present. Isaiah 9:6 tells us, "For unto us a

Child is born, unto us a Son is given." Unlike the gifts of this world, He will never change, break, or get lost, and no one can ever take Him away from us (or us from Him). Some gifts, like my brother's airplane, last only a few seconds, but Jesus Christ is quite literally the gift that keeps on giving, for all eternity.

Next time we sit down with our families to exchange gifts—whether it's for Christmas, a birthday, or whatever the occasion may be—please be reminded of the most precious and beautiful present of all, our Lord and Savior, Jesus Christ. May He be the only treasure that our hearts truly desire and seek. Thousands of years ago, wise men sought Him. Today, may wise men (and women) seek Him still.

Day 41—Father Does Best

In my early thirties I was very confused where my provision truly came from. I was working several jobs, owned a business, and had political aspirations. I felt secure in my ability to provide for my family. In other words, like Lot in Genesis 13:10, I had taken my eyes off God and had placed them on the world. Then in 2009 the bottom dropped out. My business tanked, we nearly lost our home, our savings and retirement were depleted, and our finances nose-dived. So much for relying on the world!

As everything I had worked so hard to accomplish began to quickly unravel all around me, I found myself on my face before the Lord. As those quiet times alone with my Savior became more frequent, and as I literally let go of my trust in the world system around me and placed my trust squarely on Him, the truth of my error was revealed. I realized that in my personal aspirations and ambition, I had failed to submit to God for guidance and provision. Instead, I had looked to the world and my own abilities. It was an enormous, prideful mistake on my part, but the Lord redeemed it to teach me a priceless lesson!

The truth is that ALL our provision comes from God; therefore, we don't need to strive in the flesh and stress out. In fact, in Matthew chapter 6, Jesus says in verse 25, "Do not worry about your life." In verse 31 He states, "Do not worry, saying, 'What shall we eat?' or 'What shall we drink?' or 'What shall we wear?'" And finally, in verse 34 He says, "Do not worry about tomorrow." Three times between verses 25 and 34 the Lord exhorts us not to worry about where our provision comes from. Listen, everything Jesus says is important for us to hear and obey, but when He repeats Himself, we need to pay extra special attention!

When my children were young, they never wondered whether or not I would feed, shelter, or clothe them—they *knew* I would. They had faith in me. Yet, I'm an imperfect father at best. On the other hand, our Heavenly Father is perfect and He loves us perfectly; therefore, He will provide for us perfectly as well. Remember, James 1:17 states, "Every good gift and every perfect gift is from above, and comes down from the Father." God is the One who meets our needs, not a job or another person, and certainly not ourselves. It's all God!

So our focus shouldn't be on provision, it should be on Jesus! Let's put our focus where it belongs, not on the things of this world, but on eternity, and with childlike faith let's trust our Father to do what He does best!

Day 42—Don't Blow Up Your Truck

We live in a society that is always seeking instant results. Patience is a virtue but that does not come easily to most of us! Years ago, when Juanita and I were first dating, I was in a rush to deliver her the Christmas gifts I had bought her. About a mile from my parents' house I realized my truck was overheating. I had a choice to make, so I cranked up the heater and drove thirty-five miles to Juanita's parents' house. In retrospect I should have turned around, but instead my desire to give her the presents I had so excitedly purchased for her overwhelmed my sense of reason.

Long story short, she absolutely loved her Christmas presents and I completely blew the engine in my truck! I guess you could say that was my Christmas gift to myself. My impatience cost me my truck, which sadly I was unable to afford to fix.

When we are impatient, we tend to either force things to happen in our timing instead of God's (like I did with my truck), or we lose interest and give up. Neither is a good road to tread. Paul reminds us of a better way in Galatians 6:9, which states, "And let us not grow weary while doing good, for in due season we shall reap if we do not lose heart." In other words don't give up, don't get wiped out, don't lose heart, don't get impatient—the harvest is coming!

As believers, it is important that we not force things to happen when it isn't God's perfect timing. Part of our spiritual growth is learning to trust and wait on the Lord. He knows exactly what He is doing in our lives. If we will just remain steadfast, believing that God keeps His promises, we will see incredible things happen in our lives.

Our enemy wants to see us get ripped off, to settle for second best, but God is telling us that if we will just abide in Him there will be an incredible harvest to reap! So don't blow up your truck...wait on the Lord and He will reward you in His perfect time!

Day 43—His Goodness Leads to Repentance

When I was a teenager I struggled with feelings of loneliness and depression in my life. When I was at rock bottom God blessed me with a godly friend and mentor named Boaz, who demonstrated grace, mercy, and love to me when I had done absolutely nothing to deserve it, and had nothing to offer in return. Yet this friend was still just an imperfect human being like me, which reminded me how much more does God, who *is* perfect, love and care for me! That simple realization led me to fully abandon myself in Jesus Christ.

Paul wrote in Romans 2:4, "Or do you despise the riches of His goodness, forbearance, and longsuffering, not knowing that the goodness of God leads you to repentance?" The Greek word for "leads," or *ago*, can also be translated "guides or directs, as to a specific destination," like the signs on the side of the road. God's goodness guides us to the exact point where we must make a choice to either repent or reject Him. When we repent, we literally turn away from our sins and change direction toward Jesus. But how does His goodness lead us to the point of repentance?

Simply, God's goodness, grace, mercy, and love, draw sinners to Him. When we fully appreciate the fact that Christ sacrificed Himself because He loves us so much, we also begin to realize that He did this without us deserving such sacrifice. Paul states in Romans 5:8, "But God demonstrates His own love toward us, in that while we were still sinners, Christ died for us." In other words, Christ paid the ultimate price without any of us deserving it. In light of His pure love, selflessness, and holiness, our sinful nature becomes that much more glaringly obvious and equally hideous. The lost sheep begins to realize that he is lost and in need of a Savior. When this realization of the need for salvation truly overtakes a person, the obvious choice is to repent of our sins and like the prodigal son, run straight into the arms of our loving Heavenly Father.

Even as Christians, God's goodness still leads us to repentance! Perhaps there is unresolved sin in your life. Perhaps, despite Christ's sacrifice, your pride hasn't fully allowed you to relinquish control and submit to His lordship. If you truly love Him in return, it's time to repent and cut loose those last remaining strings connecting you to your former life. Jesus said in John 10:10, "I have come that they may have life, and that they may have it more abundantly." That will only happen when we turn away from our sin and fully abandon ourselves in Jesus Christ.

Day 44—Control Freak

I had a friend once who was very controlling. This person did not like it when I would hang out with other friends from my church—even confronting me about it. I'm a very relational person and I enjoy interacting with other believers, but this person constantly tried to siphon me away from the body of Christ. He seemed to enjoy tearing down Christians who I admired because they were very solid in their faith. He also wasn't a very positive influence, getting me into a few situations of compromise that I later regretted.

Clearly it was a very unhealthy relationship and I allowed myself to put up with it far longer than I should have. It was a difficult moment when I had to finally put my foot down and tell this friend that we could no longer hang out together, but I knew it was the correct thing to do and I was relieved when it was done.

The church of Corinth was also being influenced and controlled. There were false apostles among them, men who were abusing the church by sowing seeds of discord and false doctrine—and many in the church were putting up with it! Paul writes in Second Corinthians 11:20, "For you put up with it if one brings you into bondage, if one devours you, if one takes from you, if one exalts himself, if one strikes you on the face." Instead of putting their foot down and ending the abuse and control, the church of Corinth was allowing themselves to be subject to the bondage of these wolves in sheep's clothing. They had the power to stop it, but instead they were allowing it to continue.

What about us today? False ministers, deceitful doctrines, and demonic spirits disguised as angels of light still attempt to infiltrate Christ's church, though they lost their power over us through the finished work of the cross. Nonetheless, they try to exercise illegitimate control when they have no right to do so.

As children of God and joint heirs with Christ, we do not need to put up with it! The church has been bought and paid for by the blood of Jesus Christ; we don't have to accept the abuse and control of false ministers and doctrines of demons. Today, let's purpose in our hearts to reject any of these outside influences and instead let's set our foundation on Jesus Christ and the truth of God's Word.

Day 45—Giving What We Don't Deserve

It's sobering how we behave when we're walking in the flesh and not in the Spirit. I remember this one time I was driving a company vehicle, performing building inspections for a former employer, when suddenly this huge, burly guy stepped right in front of my car as I was exiting the driveway and demanded to know why I was taking pictures of the building next door. I was already in a bad mood and there was a part of my flesh that was foolishly looking to pick a fight with this man, so I basically chewed him out. Then I waited for his angry response. Instead, his face contorted and he got teary-eyed, then he mumbled, "I was just asking a question," as he meekly shuffled away. I felt terrible. He had every right to ask his question, he could have been disrespectful back to me, and he could have probably beat me to a pulp, but instead he humbly walked away. I was ashamed the whole ride home as I meditated on the word "mercy."

Mercy can be defined as "receiving compassion or forgiveness instead of harsh treatment." Mercy is something we don't deserve; yet, it's God's mercy that allows us to come to the cross, unworthy but grateful for the gift of salvation through faith by the death and resurrection of Jesus Christ. The realization of this undeserved gift should profoundly affect who we are and how we interact with other people.

In Luke 7:47, after a notoriously sinful woman washes and wipes Jesus' feet with her tears and hair, then kisses and pours fragrant oil on them, He says, "Therefore I say to you, her sins, which are many, are forgiven, for she loved much. But to whom little is forgiven, the same loves little." We have been forgiven much; therefore, we should love much. God has poured out so much mercy upon us that we should be filled with mercy for others in return. And it is with the same measure of mercy that we have received, that we are to love those who do not deserve or return our love.

Right now, stop and think about those brothers or sisters in Christ who may be difficult to love and forgive. Next, consider all that we have done to wrong others, including our Savior, and then further consider the mercy that Christ and others have bestowed undeservedly upon us. In Luke 6:37-38, Jesus says, "Forgive, and you will be forgiven...For with the same measure that you use, it will be measured back to you." Let's not only receive mercy, but thankfully extend it to others who have not earned it as well; for that is the very heart of giving what we don't deserve ourselves.

Day 46—None Righteous

Have you ever considered the "natural" behavior of a young child? No different than an adult, a child's inherent tendency is to manifest sin. I remember years ago when my son, Maksim, was a toddler, he got into some craft paint when he thought no one was looking. Instinctively, he took the paint to his room, hid in the furthest area away from the door behind the bed (so he couldn't be seen), and proceeded to "paint" his bed, our beige carpet, and himself with, of all things, black paint! Such a scenario had never happened before (and hopefully never will again!); yet, Maksim clearly knew it was wrong and did it nonetheless. He even tried to keep his sin a secret. Who taught him to sin and then to attempt to cover up his wrongdoing?

Romans 5:12 says, "through one man [Adam] sin entered the world, and death through sin, and thus death spread to all men." As a result, our inherent sinful nature is persistently attempting to rear its ugly head and we battle against it constantly. I appreciate Paul's brutal honesty when he admits in Romans 7:15, "For what I am doing, I do not understand. For what I will to do, that I do not practice; but what I hate, that I do."

It is with the truth of mankind's inherent sinful nature in mind that Romans 3:10 clearly states, "There is none righteous, no, not one." The Greek word for "righteous" in this verse is *dikaios,* which can also be translated to mean "innocent or guiltless." Paul is saying that none of us, even on our absolute best day, is innocent of sin. On our own, we all stand guilty before the Lord.

Isaiah 64:6 says, "But we are all like an unclean thing, and all our righteousnesses are like filthy rags." God is not impressed with our self-righteousness. Our best attempts are still disgusting to Him. There is nothing, absolutely nothing we can do to save ourselves—we need a Savior!

We all need to be careful not to think more highly of ourselves than we ought to. We have no righteousness in and of ourselves. Like Paul wrote in Philippians 3:9, "not having my own righteousness, which is from the law, but that which is through faith in Christ, the righteousness which is from God by faith." True righteousness can only come through Jesus Christ. Remembering that truth should keep us both humble and appreciative of all He has done for us!

Day 47—The Nicest Tough Guy Around

When I was a kid, I was smaller than most of the other boys, so I tended to be an easy target. In every grade though, there was always one guy, Isaac, who looked out for me. He was bigger than most of the boys. Isaac was athletic, confident, and very popular. You wouldn't guess by looking at him because he was pretty intimidating, but he had a very gentle spirit, and a tender and compassionate heart. I always thought that Isaac was the nicest tough guy around because he knew when to be gentle and when to be strong.

In Second Corinthians 10:1, we read, "Now I, Paul, myself am pleading with you by the meekness and gentleness of Christ—who in presence am lowly among you, but being absent am bold toward you." Lowly and bold—they seem like two contradictory qualities, but the reality is they represent a balanced approach.

Paul was meek and gentle with the church of Corinth, but he was also bold and firm. He knew that different approaches were necessary in different circumstances, and rather than relying on himself, he was Spirit-led. The perfect example of this, of course, is Jesus Christ. Jesus is the Lamb of God and the Lion of the Tribe of Judah. He took the form of a

[107]

Servant though He is the King of Kings and the Lord of Lords.

Today, let's pray for discernment to know when to be meek and when to be bold, and how to effectively combine the two. May everything that we say and do be rooted in our love for Jesus and our love for people. As we prayerfully seek God for wisdom and direction in how we connect with others, and how to correct them when necessary, we can have confidence that He will show us the way. After all, Jesus is the perfect example of the nicest tough guy around!

Day 48—Is Christ Divided?

Back when I owned my own business I had a dispute with a former client who also was a believer. He hired me as a consultant to help mediate a disagreement between him and his landlord. I performed my side of the agreement but when it came time for him to pay me, he refused on the grounds that he had changed his mind and no longer needed my services, though I had already performed them. We met up at Starbucks to talk it over. The conversation didn't begin well—both of us were a little heated. Yet at some point, I strongly felt the Holy Spirit urging me to "release" him of his obligation to pay me, which I did. After that the entire tone of the conversation changed and as we closed in prayer, a lady who was observing nearby came up to us and asked us both to pray for her too!

Unity within the body of Christ is one of the church's greatest strengths; likewise, the lack of unity is one of our greatest weaknesses. Jesus said in Matthew 12:25, "Every kingdom divided against itself is brought to desolation, and every city or house divided against itself will not stand." Satan knows this truth which is why he works overtime to sow dissension and discord in the body of Christ. Think about that—the *body* of Christ. Can a body be divided? Or as Paul asks in First Corinthians 1:13,

"Is Christ divided?" Obviously, Christ cannot be divided.

So, if we are members of the body of Christ, and Christ cannot be divided, then neither should we be divided with one another. Ephesians 4:4-6 says:

> There is one body and one Spirit, just as you were called in one hope of your calling; one Lord, one faith, one baptism; one God and Father of all, who is above all, and through all, and in you all.

We are all different and unique; yet, there is a powerful bond that glues us together as one. It's not a founder of a movement, it's not a denomination—we have been baptized into one body by Jesus Christ! Only Jesus was crucified for our sins and it's in His name and by His blood that we are baptized into the body of Christ; therefore, our focus should always, *always* be on Him!

There are a lot of non-essential things that can divide us, but there is one all-powerful, all-knowing, ever-present God who unites us! Is Christ divided?—no, and neither should His representation to the world, His church, be. Instead, let us be united in, by, and through Him that we "may with one mind and one mouth glorify the God and Father of our Lord Jesus Christ" (Romans 15:6).

Day 49—Jesus Revealed!

I enjoy hunting for antique or vintage items that are undervalued by the seller. Recently, I found a great set of vintage lockers for an incredible price. I knew I could sell this piece for double what I paid, so after a friend helped me pick them up in his truck to get them to my house, I got right to work repairing one of the legs and cleaning the lockers. I was pretty sure I could accomplish this easily by myself—but I was wrong. The lockers were huge and super heavy, and I struggled to maneuver them so I could get my work done. Finally, when it was time to set them upright, I nearly buckled under the weight and at one point I caught the lockers on my foot and the metal carved out a chunk of my boot (thankfully not my foot with it)! So much for my attempt at doing things *my* way! It turned out I needed someone's help after all.

In essence, that is what the law accomplished—it demonstrated to mankind our profound inability to successfully earn salvation based on our own attempts at righteousness, and in the process, revealed our need for a Savior. In Romans 3:21, Paul writes, "But now the righteousness of God apart from the law is revealed, being witnessed by the Law and the Prophets." Praise God that there is righteousness *apart* from the law, not based on our own disgusting attempts at righteousness derived from works, but instead based on true and pure righteousness, which can only be found in Jesus Christ!

Consider also the beautiful truth that God designed, all along, for there to be continuity between the law and the gospel; thereby, demonstrating God's all-encompassing perfect plan for mankind's salvation. This is why Paul said in verse 21 that righteousness by faith in Christ, which is apart from the law, was "witnessed by the Law and the Prophets." The Greek word for "witnessed" is *martureo* and it means "to give testimony." This is not a passive act, like a witness seeing something and then walking away; no, this is a witness that testifies, like in a court of law! As Galatians 3:24 states, "Therefore the law was our tutor to bring us to Christ, that we might be justified by faith."

From Genesis to Revelation, as God's perfect plan is revealed, it's all about Jesus Christ! Therefore, as Christians, we ought to be careful not to become distracted by the things of this world which are passing away around us even at this very moment, and instead, keep our focus on what matters most—Jesus! Colossians 1:18 proclaims, "And He is the head of the body, the church, who is the beginning, the firstborn from the dead, that in all things He may have the preeminence." May Jesus always have the preeminence in our lives that only He deserves!

Day 50—Unlikely Heroes

Many years ago in high school, when I was first learning to play guitar, some classmates and I decided it would be fun to form a worship band. Everybody in the band was just learning how to play an instrument or sing, so needless to say we sounded awful. Not long after, I received an invitation for us to lead worship for a chapel service at a local Christian middle school and without hesitating I committed us to the event!

The night before the chapel service we gathered together to run through the set list and quickly realized that our appearance the next day would be an exercise in humility—we sounded terrible.

The next morning we were practicing at the school, hoping for a miracle as the students were filing in for their chapel service. We went in the back, huddled together, and prayed the most sincere and desperate prayer that God would be blessed by our hearts to worship Him, even if we publicly embarrassed ourselves with our lack of musical ability in the process! What occurred in the hour that followed was one of the most powerful worship times I have ever experienced in my life. In fact, so many kids came forward to either accept the Lord or rededicate their lives that the principal cancelled school for the remainder of the day.

I was reminded of First Corinthians 1:27 and 29, which says:

> But God has chosen the foolish things of the world to put to shame the wise, and God has chosen the weak things of the world to put to shame the things which are mighty...that no flesh should glory in His presence.

Later that day, as the worship band sat around the table of a local diner, we marveled at what had taken place hours before. Offhandedly, someone suggested we run through the worship set list again. Enthusiastically, we all agreed. Can you guess what happened? That's right—once again we all sounded terrible!

When we realize and embrace the truth that we're all rough around the edges and it's the Lord who is working in and through us, it's hard to get a big head. And that's the point. God doesn't want us seeking attention, fame, or glory. He doesn't want us taking credit for what the Holy Spirit accomplishes through us. The paintbrush can't take credit for the painting, the chisel can't take credit for the sculpture, and we can't take credit for the work of the Holy Spirit. We are just humble instruments in the hands of God—He alone deserves the glory!

Day 51—God's Promises Await

Have you ever wondered if God's promises no longer applied to you because of past failures? I remember when I was in high school the Lord spoke some profound promises into my life through His Word and the Holy Spirit. Then I made some poor choices and the next thing I knew, I was wallowing in guilt and self-condemnation, fully convinced that I had eradicated God's promises. For a long time I existed in that defeated mindset, afraid to fail again. I was behaving as if my works could somehow justify me before God.

In Romans 4:2-3, Paul writes:

> For if Abraham was justified by works, he has something to boast about, but not before God. For what does the Scripture say? "Abraham believed God, and it was accounted to him for righteousness."

In Hebrews 11, which many refer to as the "Faith Hall of Fame," Abraham is named multiple times for being a man of faith. Fortunately for Abraham, he was *not* justified based on his works because from that standpoint he failed notably numerous times.

In Genesis 15:5-6, God tells Abram (eventually changed to Abraham):

"Look now toward heaven, and count the stars if you are able to number them." And He said to him, "So shall your descendants be." And he believed in the Lord, and He accounted it to him for righteousness.

The Hebrew word for "believed" is *aman*, which means to "confirm or trust," and it shares the same root as the word *amen*, which means "so be it." In other words, Abraham was fully committed to the Lord. The point that Paul is making is that Abraham was justified because of the faith he had in the Lord, not in his works. By his works Abraham sowed to the flesh and failed multiple times. Yet, God still kept His promises to Abraham and although Abraham's faith in certain circumstances sometimes faltered, his ultimate faith in God did not.

Are you beating yourself up over past mistakes and now you are wondering if God will still keep His promises to you? Let me remind you that His promises are not based on our performance—they are gifts of grace that we receive through faith. Remember, Abraham was not a perfect man, but he believed God and "it was accounted to him for righteousness." It's time for us also to believe and move forward to the future—God's promises await us!

Day 52—Faithful, Not Famous

As I look back on my life, I see the influence of many godly people, but the four men that stand out from the rest are the ones that the Lord anointed to demonstrate to me what it means to be a godly man. The first is my father, who has shown me what it means to be hardworking, patient, and generous, always placing the Lord and his family before himself. The second man was my elementary school teacher, now a pastor, who was a friend to me when I felt I had none. He showed me the power of humility and love. The third man was my former business partner and friend, who taught me what it means to step out in faith and trust the Lord for provision and protection, and to be a good steward of all God's blessings. The fourth man is my pastor who possesses all the qualities of the aforementioned three men and has demonstrated how to apply those qualities to living kingdom-minded for the glory of God, for the equipping of the saints, and with a heart for the lost.

I intentionally left out their names because their hearts are to be faithful, not famous. We see this in Second Corinthians 8:16-24, when Paul writes concerning Titus and an unnamed "brother" who together ministered to the church in Corinth. There is plenty of conjecture and speculation concerning who this anonymous brother is, but Paul, at the leading of the Holy Spirit, does not name him. However, Paul does say, "And we have sent with him the brother whose praise is in the gospel throughout all the churches" (2 Corinthians 8:18). His name wasn't important, but here's what was important—he was praiseworthy and trustworthy. In other words, he was a faithful brother.

It doesn't matter if we get credit, thanks, or accolades for the things we do for the Lord; all that matters is that He knows and He is pleased. People may not even be fully aware who we are; yet, they are impacted by the influence that God calls us to for His glory and for His kingdom. Jesus said in Matthew 6:3-4:

> But when you do a charitable deed, do
> not let your left hand know what your
> right hand is doing, that your charitable
> deed may be in secret; and your Father
> who sees in secret will Himself reward
> you openly.

We've all been touched or blessed by someone, and they may not even know it. Likewise, we're impacting people left and right, and probably don't even fully realize to what extent. Today, may we be like the unnamed brother—committed to being faithful and not concerned with being famous.

Day 53—From Weaklings to Warriors

I am a living testimony of Christ's miraculous work in a broken life. Looking back, I can only boast in His amazing love and grace. You see, I was a painfully introverted person in my youth. After years of being teased and rejected, I could barely hold a conversation or look someone in the eye. I didn't like being around people and I preferred to be alone. There were walls up all over my life, which were meant to protect me, but they only isolated me further. I was afraid to even take a chance of being vulnerable because that meant potentially more hurt and pain, of which I already had my fair share. I was broken, weary, and afraid.

The good thing about hitting rock bottom is there's nowhere to look but up. I still remember the exact moment that I fully surrendered my life to Christ. It wasn't anything noble on my part—I didn't have much of a life to surrender anyway. It was like giving your best friend the most broken toy you've got—but that's all I had. Amazingly, that's all He wanted.

Paul knew what it was to be broken. Like a glass man, thrown at a solid rock, he was obliterated into pieces. But he learned, as we all hopefully do at some point in our lives, that God doesn't do that to keep us broken—He does it so He can build us back up again.

Once we are out of the way, once our expectations, opinions, egos, and agendas are decimated, once we fully surrender and let go of what we hold so dear, then He is free to mold us into the masterpieces He desires us to become. And so Paul could honestly admit, "God forbid that I should boast except in the cross of our Lord Jesus Christ" (Galatians 6:14).

People appreciate demonstrations. It's the reason why car dealers allow us to test drive their vehicles and clothing stores have dressing rooms. Do we want to see a demonstration of the power of the Holy Spirit? Let's honestly examine our own lives. Apart from God we are full of weakness and inability, but when we are fully surrendered to Him, "we are more than conquerors through Him who loved us" (Romans 8:37).

God isn't impressed by power and persuasion; He's looking for broken people, like Paul, like us, who will fully surrender their weakness to Him. Because when a weakling becomes a warrior, and the lightbulb finally clicks as we catch a glimpse in the mirror of the masterpiece our Savior is creating, then we can fully give Him all the glory He deserves.

Day 54—Marked!

Back in the days when I worked for county government, I was blessed to have several promotions which allowed me the opportunity to relocate to different offices. One of those relocations occurred right before my annual two-week vacation, and the move was to our central headquarters in San Bernardino.

I remember returning from a relaxing vacation and immediately setting up shop in a corner office at "central." However, right off the bat people began treating me differently—almost with reverence. It was weird. So I asked a good friend of mine what was going on. I was stunned by his answer. No one knew about my promotion or relocation, so everyone thought one day I must have been fed up, decided to pack my stuff, and snagged a corner office at the main headquarters! I had been marked by my coworkers as gutsy and bold, when in reality I was none of those things and it was all a big misunderstanding! Nevertheless, that reputation followed me the entire time I was there.

Likewise, the qualities and character traits that "mark" us as Christians are also evident to all—for better or worse. And as followers of Jesus Christ, our lives should be marked by wisdom, not foolishness. Wisdom isn't just about *what* we know; it's about *how* we apply what we know, and it all begins with *who* we know! James 1:5 says, "If any of you lacks wisdom, let him ask of God, who gives to all liberally and without reproach, and it will be given to him." Saved people should be the wisest people on the planet because God has made wisdom available to us through His Son, Jesus Christ! You see, Christians should not have a reputation for foolish behavior; instead, Christians should be marked by their wisdom. In doing so, we "walk worthy of the calling with which [we] were called" (Ephesians 4:1).

Let's truthfully consider the qualities that mark our lives as believers. Are we known for being wise, or are we known for our foolish behavior and poor decisions? Do we demonstrate a life lived well or poorly? Do we attract people to Jesus by walking worthy of our calling, or do we push people away? God's Word is clear—Jesus Christ is our eternal source of wisdom! That means we have every resource available to us to make wise decisions and to live life well. In other words, we literally have no excuse for foolishness! So today, let's purpose in our hearts to be marked as a people known for godly wisdom—a people marked by our precious Savior.

Day 55—Rome Didn't Fall in a Day

When I was a young adult, I had an incredible opportunity to work over the summer at a Christian camp in the mountains of Idyllwild, CA. I was thrilled about the opportunity to serve and seek the Lord surrounded by His beautiful creation and His people! But as I was preparing to go, my best friend prophetically warned me that I would meet a girl at the camp and I was not to begin a dating relationship with her because doing so would eventually result in my falling away from the Lord. I quickly dismissed his warning because dating was the furthest thing from my mind. I was going on a spiritual journey; I wasn't looking for a girlfriend!

Well, long story short, I did meet a girl that summer and although I initially deflected her attention, I eventually gave in and we began dating. True to my friend's warning, the relationship became a great distraction in my walk with Christ and I did eventually find myself in a dark place where I had indeed fallen away from the Lord.

Every alcoholic has their first seemingly innocent drink and every adulterer has their first "double-take" at the person who isn't their spouse. We've all heard the saying, "Rome wasn't built in a day." Well, Rome didn't fall in a day either. The moral failures of our lives often begin with what appear to be innocent compromises. Ephesians 4:27 reminds us that we are not to "give place to the devil." Many of the choices we make have the potential to allow our enemy a foothold in our lives. A thief doesn't need your front door to be left wide open to rob you—he just needs it left unlocked. First Peter 5:8 states, "Be sober, be vigilant; because your adversary the devil walks about like a roaring lion, seeking whom he may devour."

As Christians, we need not live in fear of the devil, but it would be equally unwise to underestimate him. After all, he has had many millennia to craft his art. He wants to destroy us, he wants to destroy our relationships, and the ultimate relationship he wants to destroy is the relationship between us and the Lord.

Today, let's decide not to give the devil any opportunity that he can take advantage of or exploit in our lives. We need to be on our guard, aware, and leaning on Christ for our strength. The enemy is looking for a weakness, an "unlocked door" in our lives. It's our choice whether we give it to him or not.

Day 56—The Way of Grace

I am thankful God allowed me the privilege of owning a business for six years because it taught me valuable skills and gave me a burden for the marketplace. Still, I have to admit that my motivation for leaving my prior property management job was nothing more than selfish pride. You see, I had just completed a two-year long, self-initiated project to get the streets and sidewalks replaced in a sprawling property I managed in Colton. When the project was completed, I had helped procure over $300,000 of improvements without it costing my employer a penny. When I presented the completed project I was disappointed when the only reaction I received was a congratulatory e-mail. I remember thinking, *I did all that work for two years and they barely even cared!* They owed me something for saving them all that money. It was then that I decided to leave and open my own business.

We live in a works-based world. We study hard in school to get good grades, we exercise in the gym so our bodies will be healthy, and we go to our jobs knowing we will be paid for our time. However, people cross into dangerous territory when they think they can apply this same strategy to earn eternal salvation through works of self-righteousness.

Romans 4:14 says, "For if those who are of the law are heirs, faith is made void and the promise made of no effect." When we begin to believe that our good works make us worthy of salvation, we not only void the value of faith, we also create a false reality that God is in debt to us because He now owes us what we have rightfully earned. Nothing could be further from the truth! Ephesians 2:8-9 states, "For by grace you have been saved through faith, and that not of yourselves; it is the gift of God, not of works, lest anyone should boast."

If God gave us what we actually deserved, trust me, you would not want it because what we deserve is eternal death (Romans 6:23). Instead, He gives us what we do *not* deserve—a gift of grace by faith—the gift of eternal life with Him. We should be thankful to God that we are not paid the wages we have earned.

We need to be a people who demonstrate grace to others—when we do, our lives reflect Christ. First John 2:6 says, "He who says he abides in Him ought himself also to walk just as He walked." The Greek word for "walk" is *peripateo* which can also be translated "to live." We need to *live* like Jesus lived! The world tells us we are owed based on our works, but God shows us a better way—the way of grace.

Day 57—Not a Loan, It's a Gift

As many people experienced, the last half of the first decade of the twenty-first century was pretty rough financially. My family was no exception and so due to reasons beyond our control, we fell behind on our mortgage. It was a miracle and answer to prayer that despite being ten months behind, through a combination of multiple blessings, we were able to get nine of the months caught up—but we were still short one month.

So the Lord put it on my heart to reach out to a close friend for a loan. I prayed it over, thought it through, and then I presented him with my request, along with a repayment schedule, modest interest, and a valuable ring as collateral. I was blessed when he responded positively, but I was shocked and humbled when he said that it wouldn't be a loan, but a gift of $1,500. Praise God, with that final piece we paid off our back payments to the bank and became current on the mortgage.

The author of Hebrews writes, "But do not forget to do good and to share, for with such sacrifices God is well pleased" (Hebrews 13:16). One of the most powerful ways we can demonstrate the sincerity of our love is by giving to one another. It is a powerful testimony and example of the depths of our commitment and love within the body of Christ.

Why? Because in doing so we resemble our Heavenly Father; we reflect His image as we display His heart of giving and love. We see this truth in James 1:17, which states, "Every good gift and every perfect gift is from above, and comes down from the Father of lights." Giving is powerful, it can change lives, and it can bless people in ways that we can't even begin to fathom. That is what sincerely giving based on a genuine heart of agape love can do.

I always knew that my good friend cared about me and my family, but I had no idea how much he truly loved us until the moment I genuinely needed his help. First John 3:17 tells us, "whoever has this world's goods, and sees his brother in need, and shuts up his heart from him, how does the love of God abide in him?" My friend could have taken my offer and even made some extra money out of the deal. Instead, he used it as an opportunity to demonstrate his love for us.

Today, let's pray to see opportunities to give of ourselves to others and for the boldness to act. Let's not hold back from those we love, but let's give them our time, attention, affections, and financial blessings. Giving—it's one of the most loving things we can do!

Day 58—Just Accept It!

On my 37th birthday one of my best friends presented me with a gift that was ridiculously valuable! You see, I've had my Bible since I got married and so it contains all those years of notes, thoughts, and observations. It dawned on me that my Bible would be a wonderful treasure to one day pass on to my children. So to better protect it for posterity, I wanted to have it rebound in genuine leather. However, I didn't have the financial resources to do so. It was a nice thought that I tucked away in the back of my mind, but I didn't actually think it would ever happen. So imagine my surprise when my friend and dear brother in Christ told me that my birthday present was my newly rebound Bible! This was an expensive, undeserved gift, and I genuinely struggled with being receptive to the fact that it was now mine—all I had to do was accept it.

Like a valuable gift that we do not deserve, the Spirit and the things of the Spirit are also freely given to us. Second Peter 1:3 says, "His divine power has given to us all things that pertain to life and godliness." Isn't God generous? He gives us so much: salvation, eternal life, the Holy Spirit, spiritual gifts, spiritual wisdom, and much, much more. We don't deserve any of them and sometimes that can mess with us as our insecurities and pride cause us to struggle with accepting the fact that we have freely received incredible gifts! Yet, God wants us to accept with joy and purpose all the wonderful things He has freely given to us.

My children have always loved ice cream. When they were young, if someone they knew offered them ice cream, they would readily accept it—no questions asked! With joy they would accept the gift and hungrily scarf it down, even if their little tummies were already full. That eagerness and trust are qualities that Jesus referenced when He said, "Assuredly, I say to you, whoever does not receive the kingdom of God as a little child will by no means enter it" (Mark 10:15). Jesus has given us something far better than ice cream—He has given us the Holy Spirit and all that the Spirit brings. Embrace that fact like a little kid and run with it!

Perhaps our enemy has been beating you up lately—lying to you about your future, your spiritual worth, your usefulness in ministry, and your value to the body of Christ. Reject the devil and his lies! The truth is that we have freely been given God's Spirit of power, boldness, courage, and wisdom. Through the Spirit we have access to the deeper things of God. Therefore, with eagerness and excitement, let's gladly be receptive to all the wonderful things that our Heavenly Father bestows on us. It's a gift...just accept it!

Day 59—Gazing Across Your Jordan

Have you ever waited for a promise to be fulfilled that God gave you and it seemed like you were waiting forever? I'm reminded of all the years I waited for the day when I would finally meet my beautiful wife, Juanita. As a youth, I looked forward to being married one day. Growing up, I gave the marriage covenant much thought, prayer, and preparation. I knew in my heart that the Lord had given me a high regard for marriage, even as a very young man, because He was preparing me for the Promised Land of marriage. Yet, as the years passed, I became increasingly discouraged. I remember at one point, finally having an epiphany and confessing to the Lord, *I have been too preoccupied with searching for my wife. It's time I focused on You instead.* About two months after I got my priorities straight, I met Juanita!

In the first chapter of the book of Joshua, forty years after the exodus and wandering through the wilderness, the children of Israel were finally about to enter their Promised Land. In verse 11, Joshua commands his officers, "Within three days you will cross over this Jordan, to go in to possess the land which the Lord your God is giving you to possess." After all those years, they were now about to cross over the Jordan River, the final barrier that stood between them and entering the land of promise.

Are you standing on the banks of your own personal Jordan, gazing across the water at the Promised Land on the other side? Is it so close that not only can you see it, but you can hear it, smell it, almost even touch it; yet, it still seems far out of your reach? Let me ask you a question: is your focus on the Promised Land or the Faithful One who made the promise? We all need to examine ourselves carefully and honestly because I believe sometimes we confuse the two. God gives us awesome gifts, not so we can get wrapped up in the gift, but so we can give glory and praise to the Giver! Jesus said it best in Matthew 6:33, when He stated, "But seek first the kingdom of God and His righteousness, and all these things shall be added to you."

Let me encourage you, God will keep His promises and they will be fulfilled in His perfect timing. If you're wondering why it's taking so long, check your heart because there may be some issues that He wants to work out of you first. Or maybe He just wants to teach you patience! No matter what His reasons are, know, just like the children of Israel, that God has *not* forgotten His promises to you. Remember, He is called "Faithful and True" (Revelation 19:11). Guess what? That's not just a statement of fact…it's another promise, too!

Day 60—Dressing Up

I've shared before that when my son, Maksim, was younger he enjoyed dressing just like me. Well, some years back I officiated a wedding ceremony for some dear friends in which they gave him the honor of being the ring bearer and the highlight for him was we both wore nearly identical gray suits. I have a picture of Maksim and me on the day of that wedding. He's standing in front of me, my hands on his shoulders, and both of us have the biggest grins.

Dressing like me made Maksim feel grown up that day. He walked taller, had more confidence, he stood patiently with all the groomsmen during the duration of the service, and hit his cue perfectly when it was time to bring me the rings. The funny thing is the week before at Men's Wearhouse he didn't want to take off his grungy t-shirt and shorts to get fitted for the suit. He initially resisted, but once he had it on, he glowed and didn't want to take it off.

As Christians, we should have the same desire to resemble our Heavenly Father, to put on the new clothes He offers us. The clothing that God has for us is the new life we now live in Christ. Just like tossing out an old garment that is worn and frayed, we need to throw out our former life of sin in the garbage, and put on the new life of righteousness that

Jesus Christ offers us. Ephesians 4:22-24 states it like this:

> Put off, concerning your former conduct, the old man which grows corrupt according to the deceitful lusts, and be renewed in the spirit of your mind, and that you put on the new man which was created according to God, in true righteousness and holiness.

Every moment of every day, let's embrace the new life that Jesus Christ has bought for us. Paul tells us in Romans 13:12, "The night is far spent, the day is at hand. Therefore let us cast off the works of darkness, and let us put on the armor of light." We no longer need to walk around in soiled and stinking garments of sin; instead, we can experience the joy of wearing brand new clothing that resembles and reflects our Heavenly Father!

Day 61—Beautiful Timing

When I first met my wife, Juanita, I had a strong feeling we would get married one day, and so within three months of dating we started talking about marriage. I was ready, but I didn't consider the possibility that she wasn't. As we started to make wedding plans, she began to withdraw from me emotionally. I knew something was wrong and I desperately tried to figure out what it was. I sensed I was losing her, so in an attempt to salvage the relationship I cancelled the wedding, but that didn't solve the problem because a week later she broke up with me anyway.

As Christians, we need to remember that the "pink slip" of our lives belongs to the Lord and He's the one who calls the shots. Proverbs 19:21 says, "There are many plans in a man's heart, nevertheless the Lord's counsel—that will stand." And of course Proverbs 16:9 reminds us, "A man's heart plans his way, but the Lord directs his steps." The calendar of our lives is not our own, but rather it must be approved by the upper management of heaven.

A wise friend once told me, "You don't want to be where the Lord doesn't want you to be." When God's calendar becomes our calendar, we can truly say as Solomon did in Ecclesiastes 3:11, "He has made everything beautiful in its time." I can say with confidence that everything works out exactly as it's supposed to when the calendar of our lives is in submission to God's perfect will.

Let's take time today to reflect on all the goals, aspirations, plans, and timetables that we face, and lay those all down before the throne of heaven. Let's surrender one of the most precious gifts we have—*time*—to the Lord and see what He does with it! God knows what He's doing in our lives and His plans are far better than our own. I learned this firsthand because Juanita and I did eventually get married, back in 1999…in God's perfect, beautiful timing.

Day 62—It's All About Jesus

I'll admit it—I love taking communion! When I take the bread, I slowly grind it under my teeth. It reminds me that Christ's body was broken for me—my sins drove Him to the cross. When I drink the juice, I savor it in my mouth. It reminds me of the sweetness of my salvation because of His blood that was shed for me. Communion is a beautiful reminder of how much He loves me and the price that He paid for that love. When I take communion, it's a time of remembrance and reflection.

In looking at Acts 2:42, we see that communion was a staple of the early church. "And they continued steadfastly in the apostles' doctrine and fellowship, in the breaking of bread, and in prayers." The term "breaking of bread" speaks of communion. God wants us to remember what He has done for us because He never wants us to forget how much He loves us. He also never wants us to forget that everything about our salvation is all because of Him. Hebrews 9:26 states, "He has appeared to put away sin by the sacrifice of Himself."

It's easy to become complacent in our knowledge of our salvation. It becomes "normal." Taking communion and remembering what Christ has done for us refreshes our memory of the sacrifice of our Savior on the cross and the majesty of His

[137]

resurrection. The miracle of salvation by grace becomes powerful and the depths of His love once again become awe-inspiring and unfathomable.

Sometimes, we can make the error of believing we can't take communion because we are struggling with temptation or sin in our lives. However, those are the times we most need to be reminded of the cross. First Corinthians 11:28 says, "But let a man examine himself, and so let him eat of the bread and drink of the cup." An honest self-examination will always draw us to Christ, as we realize our own inadequacy and shortcomings are overshadowed by His perfect love and grace.

So what is communion to us? Is it an empty ritual or a meaningless act? It doesn't have to be. Instead, I pray that we would see communion as a way to keep Jesus at the center of everything—to keep our focus on Christ and the finished work of the cross.

Day 63—It's A Team Effort

One of my greatest joys as a husband and father is to work together as a family. There is something about gathering together for a common purpose with your loved ones that just fills my heart with joy. Back when he was a little boy, I would especially get a kick out of my son, Maksim. If I was pulling weeds, he would usually be digging a random hole in the dirt next to me. If I was watering plants, he would be spraying himself in the face with the hose! If I was clearing rocks, he would be throwing rocks.

One time, Maksim was helping me wash an old Chevy truck I owned and he happened to stumble backwards and fell into a bucket filled with cold water. He was so little at the time that he was actually fully immersed up to his chin, and his little body was such a perfect fit for the bucket that he got stuck and it took me several attempts to pop him back out! That was my "little man." I loved having him there working by my side (and I still do)!

Second Corinthians 6:1 tells us, "We then, as workers together with Him also plead with you." The Greek word for "workers together" is *sunergeo* which means to "partner in labor" or "put forth power together." It's amazing to me that Jesus Christ has chosen to work through His people—ordinary, common men and women—to reach those who don't know Him with the gospel and to minister to His church. When the people of God partner in labor, we put forth power together! But notice verse 1 says that we are "workers together with Him." There is no power or even true partnership between any of us apart from Jesus Christ. He is our power and He is the bond, the glue that holds us together as we work to reach the world for Him.

Today, let's joyfully put forth our best team effort, fueled by the power of the Holy Spirit, compelled by our love for Jesus Christ, and eager to impact those around us for His kingdom. However, in all things let's never forget it's because of the grace of God that He chooses to use us to get His work done. May we never forget that our labor is all for Him, it's not about us, and we desperately need Him as our most important partner to do it successfully! It's a team effort, guys—let's get to work!

Day 64—Community, Unity, and a Flat Tire

Isn't it discouraging when an unforeseen financial need arises at just the wrong time when there is no money to resolve the problem? I remember once when we were on our way to dropping off our children at school and we suddenly heard a strange noise coming from the rear of the car. When we pulled over to investigate, I saw that one of the rear tires was flat. By the time we got to Maksim's school, the tire was toast and we were stuck. Fortunately, one of my best friends in Christ worked at that school and he helped me install the spare tire.

Afterwards, Juanita and I went to breakfast and both of us felt very down because we did not have the money to replace the tire. In fact, the other three tires were bald with wires exposed, so really we needed to replace all four tires. We wondered where we would find the funds to pay for all those tires.

When we got home, I noticed a text from my friend's wife telling me to meet at a tire shop the very next day. A distress call had gone out concerning our need and about a dozen members of the church family were chipping in to buy us four brand new tires!

There is something special about giving collectively that brings people together in the body of Christ. We see an example of this in First Corinthians 16:1—"Now concerning the collection for the saints, as I have given orders to the churches of Galatia, so you must do also." Paul is referencing how the Gentile believers were ministering to the Jewish believers in a time of famine by taking a collection, above and beyond, for those saints. He then instructs the church of Corinth to do the same. It was an opportunity for the Gentile believers to bless their brothers and sisters in Christ who lived in Jerusalem. In doing so, a simple act of giving went a long way to create community and unity in the body of Christ.

Juanita, Skylar, Maksim, and I felt so loved by that simple act of giving from our brothers and sisters in Christ. It's funny, to this very day most of those individuals still remain anonymous and yet that experience continues to remind us how our church family truly is a family that is there in times of need. I'm reminded that people really care about us, that in times of difficulty we are not alone, and that this is our family, our home.

Every day we have an opportunity to witness the community and unity that we can build through a simple act of collective giving. So let's give big and let's give generously with a cheerful heart because God can use even a flat tire to bring the body of Christ together!

Day 65—Partners in Promises

Years ago, I purchased a 1975 Chevy pickup truck and from the very first day it was quite an adventure! I needed a truck and my budget was tight, so I knew it would be an older "project" vehicle. Still, I had no idea what I was getting myself into. In the first two months of owning the truck the muffler fell off on the freeway, a tire went flat, when I took the key out of the ignition the engine wouldn't turn off, it had multiple leaks—you get the idea!

There was even a point when I tried to adjust the front bumper brackets because the bumper was pushed right up against the truck body. I got underneath and was surprised by what I saw! Someone had welded the bumper brackets to the frame (they're supposed to be bolted on instead). There was no way of telling where the brackets ended and the frame began. The brackets and the frame had become one.

Second Peter 1:4 tells us that we have been given "exceedingly great and precious promises, that through these you may be partakers of the divine nature." The Greek word for "partakers" is *koinonos* which can also be translated "partner" or "companion." When we stand on and appropriate God's wonderful promises to us, we aren't just casual observers; no, we become *active* participants in the promises—we are partners. Just like two pieces of metal that have been welded together, we become one.

How does appropriating God's promises bring us closer to Him? By making us more like Him! Romans 8:29 states, "For whom He foreknew, He also predestined to be conformed to the image of His Son." The Greek word for "image" is *eikon* which means "likeness" or "resemblance." By partnering with God in appropriating His promises, we are being transformed to resemble our precious Savior.

God's promises are tied to the importance of His Word. Psalm 138:2 proclaims, "For You have magnified Your word above all Your name." God keeps His Word and He will never break His promises. Revelation 19:11 tells us that Jesus is "called Faithful and True." Here's the key—God keeps His promises because they are who He is!

When we cling to God's promises, we cling to His very nature. We see Him for who He is and we are transformed by being in His very presence. Appropriating His promises draws us closer to Him and transforms our lives to reflect the likeness of Christ. As we become partners in promises, we become one with our Savior through His Word.

Day 66—All Means All

There was a season in my early days of ministry when I worked part-time at a local Christian camp. The end of the season had come and it was my last week of employment. On my last day, I overheard two other employees talking about how everyone was going to be receiving a bonus. Of course, my thought was that I wouldn't get the bonus because I was leaving. I was a little disappointed, but it seemed unrealistic that I would get a bonus on my last day of employment. Imagine my pleasant surprise when I did in fact receive the bonus after all! When I asked why I had still received it, I was told, "You're part of us and we ALL got the bonus."

Second Corinthians 5:14-15 says, "For the love of Christ compels us, because we judge thus: that if One died for all, then all died; and He died for all." The Greek word for "all" is *pas* which means "all, every, the whole." In other words, all means all. Jesus Christ died for everyone because everyone was dead in their sins. Christ died for the whole, not just some. He even died for those who would reject Him. Now why would Jesus die for everyone, knowing that not everyone would receive Him and accept His gift of eternal life? The answer is there in verse 14—"the love of Christ."

Let's collectively pray that the love of Christ would compel us in everything that we say or do. Second Peter 3:9 tells us, "The Lord is not slack concerning His promise, as some count slackness, but is longsuffering toward us, not willing that any should perish but that all should come to repentance." This is the heart of God—that the world would be saved through Him.

May our entire perspective of humanity be transformed by the enormity of Christ's love for the world. Jesus Christ died for all. Let's not exclude others or elevate ourselves as if He has a heart only for some. His compassion is great and His love is perfect. May everything we do, for everyone we do it, be rooted and compelled by the love of Jesus Christ. No one is outside His reach because His death is able to save all those who come to Him.

Day 67—Preach It, Vickie!

I went to Christian school throughout my entire childhood, but not all my classmates were Christians. Some were self-avowed atheists and others even toyed with the occult, even though every day we studied the Word of God in class. All schools have cliques and one such group at my high school were those who dressed all in black and seemed to have a fascination with darkness and death.

Well, during my first semester as a freshman in secular college, I ran into one of those former classmates in a philosophy class. Her name was Vickie and though we had only been acquaintances in high school, in that unfamiliar environment, we gravitated toward what was familiar—each other. As expected, the professor eventually turned the subject to worldly philosophies about God. In my personal observations, Vickie had never seemed to pay any attention or show any interest in Bible class, so I was stunned one day when she turned around in her seat and said to me, "Erik, what he's saying about God isn't true. Jesus said, 'I am the way, the truth, and the life!'"

Paul wrote in First Thessalonians 1:5, "For our gospel did not come to you in word only, but also in power, and in the Holy Spirit and in much assurance." There is power in the gospel. That is why it is so vital that we share it! It doesn't matter if the people you share the "good news" with act like they aren't listening or don't care. We can't judge the effectiveness of the gospel solely by people's immediate reactions to it because we may just be planting seeds. What people do with those seeds is between them and God, and sometimes those seeds flourish years after they've been planted. As Isaiah 55:11 proclaims, "So shall My word be that goes forth from My mouth; it shall not return to Me void, but it shall accomplish what I please, and it shall prosper in the thing for which I sent it."

Imagine what would happen if we all prayed for boldness to preach the gospel to friends, family members, coworkers, classmates, neighbors, or even strangers who do not yet know Jesus Christ. We have the good news that Jesus paid the penalty for our sins and redeemed us so that mankind can once again have fellowship with God! Let's not keep this to ourselves—let's preach it! When we share the gospel with others, we never know how or when they will soften their hearts to accept it, but one thing is for sure—like Vickie, they will never forget it! We just never know how God's Word will impact someone's life today.

Day 68—Born to Destroy the Devil's Misdeeds

Have you ever had a dream that was so scary that you were relieved to wake up and discover it was only a dream? I remember I had a dream once, where I had left church and fallen asleep while driving, only to suddenly wake up in the mountains after almost hitting a pedestrian! I remember being confused how I ended up so far from home. Then it hit me—I was supposed to be home hours ago! My family would be missing me and worried about my whereabouts. I remember waking up in a panic only to thankfully realize it was all just a dream. Whew! It reminded me of the saying, "If you don't know where you're going, you will never get there" and may I add, you could end up somewhere you *don't* want to be instead!

In contrast, God is never lost, confused, or on the wrong path. He knows exactly where He is going and how to get there! We can see this truth evident in the birth of Christ. Jesus was born with a specific plan and purpose. First John 3:8 lists one of His purposes when John writes, "He who sins is of the devil, for the devil has sinned from the beginning. For this purpose the Son of God was manifested, that He might destroy the works of the devil." We see this purpose first documented approximately 1,500 years before the birth of Christ, when Moses recorded the words of God to the serpent in Genesis 3:15, stating, "And I will put enmity between you and the woman, and between your seed and her Seed; He shall bruise your head, and you shall bruise His heel."

Lest we underestimate the severity of the word "bruise," another translation of the Hebrew word *shuwph* is "to crush." Having your heel crushed is not lethal, but having your head crushed most definitely is. I remember as a little kid growing up, many summers we would find rattlesnakes in our backyard. Whenever we found one, my dad would always go straight for its head. A swift blow to the head would crush the rattlesnake's skull and kill it before it could strike first. So dating all the way back to the fall of man, God was giving the devil advance notice that a Savior was coming to deliver him a lethal blow to the head that would crush him and end his misdeeds once and for all!

Doesn't it fill you with confidence and peace to know that Jesus Christ, our Savior and Lord, is working everything out according to a specific plan and purpose? Jesus was born to crush the devil's head and to gain victory over sin and death. So whenever we feel confused or uncertain, let's hold fast to the truth that God does not suffer from confusion or uncertainty—unlike us, He knows exactly what He is doing!

[150]

Day 69—I'm Falling Apart

Lately, I'm being reminded how easily our physical bodies deteriorate. My hair is not as thick as it used to be and my knees regularly ache. My vision has worsened, too. The other day I took my glasses off for a second while driving on a deserted road and panicked when I came near a dark shape that I couldn't clearly see (it turned out to be an oil stain). My right index finger spasms all the time now. The doctors call it *focal dystonia* and there is no cure, so I am typing this devo with my thumb, but now I'm starting to lose control of my thumb! I have various aches and pains, which is strange because I've never played a contact sport in my life. I exercise regularly, have a healthy diet, and I'm still falling apart!

Thankfully, this physical body is only temporary. We are told in James 4:14, "For what is your life? It is even a vapor that appears for a little time and then vanishes away." Thankfully, one day these earthly bodies will be upgraded to a new heavenly body. No more index finger that thinks for itself, no more knee that pops every time I bend it, no more eyeglasses to fumble for on the nightstand. Instead of a weathered tent, I'll have a heavenly house for eternity.

Right this very moment there are many within the body of Christ who may be struggling through health issues or a disability. Be encouraged that in the context of eternity, these physical setbacks are only temporary. Paul writes in Romans 8:18, "For I consider that the sufferings of this present time are not worthy to be compared with the glory which shall be revealed in us." I sure look forward to that day, don't you?

Today, let's find peace and hope, knowing that God has greater plans for us and shedding these tattered tents is only one of them! One day, we will be in heaven with our Lord.

> And God will wipe away every tear from their eyes; there shall be no more death, nor sorrow, nor crying. There shall be no more pain, for the former things have passed away. Then He who sat on the throne said, 'Behold, I make all things new.' (Revelation 21:4-5)

Our bodies might be slowly falling apart here, but He has something much better planned for us there!

Day 70—Divine Distributor

When I was a kid, there were all kinds of jobs I wanted to have when I grew up: a fireman, C.I.A. agent, movie director, Air Force pilot, and professional baseball player, just to name a few. However, I never felt particularly talented in anything and this was especially true when it came to sports. Do you remember in P.E. when two kids would be designated as "team captains" and then each would take turns choosing their team? Well, I was always the last one picked for teams because nobody ever wanted me on their team. A classmate with a broken leg and crutches would get picked before I would! It seemed that every talent I wanted to have was instead given to somebody else.

Praise God, when it comes to our role on the team of the body of Christ, we all have a unique part to play. Romans 12:5-6 says, "so we, being many, are one body in Christ, and individually members of one another. Having then gifts differing according to the grace that is given to us, let us use them." Each one of us has been given at least one gift of the Spirit that we might edify the rest of the body of Christ. Therefore, it's a good thing to desire spiritual gifts, but ultimately it is God's choice what gifting He will bless us with. First Peter 4:10 states, "As each one has received a gift, minister it to one another, as good stewards of the manifold grace of God." God is the one who gives us the gifts of the Spirit and He's the one who decides which gifts to give.

Perhaps you have been discouraged lately because you are trying to figure out where you fit into the body of Christ. I pray you will be encouraged today. Scripture teaches that every believer has been given gifts of the Spirit that God has distributed to each of us individually. It may not necessarily be the gift you've desired, but do you trust that God's plans are better than your own? Don't allow Satan to rob you of the joy that God has prepared just for you.

Think about how amazing it is that the gifts God has given you, He handpicked to match you perfectly! You see, I eventually realized I was never designed to be good at sports, but the Lord revealed other talents He gave me instead. How much more is this true with the gifts of the Spirit? Don't focus on the gifts you don't have; instead, focus on the gifts you do have. Even better, focus on the Divine Distributor who gives the gifts! Remember, God gives us exactly what we need. Today, be blessed to know that you serve a unique role in the body of Christ, for He has gifted you and empowered you for such a time as this…

Day 71—Garage Sale Treasure

Juanita and I enjoy spending our Friday mornings visiting garage sales, looking for interesting, unique, or valuable items. One particular day it was already late in the morning, which usually means the best finds are long gone. In fact, we had already picked up Maksim from school, when we saw a sign on the way home and decided to stop at one last house.

The yard sale had been picked pretty clean, but you never know what you might find when you dig. Juanita came across a stamp album with a water-damaged, detached cover and stamps floating everywhere—it was a mess! Before we even asked, the owner of the home jumped in and said we could have the album, so we went ahead and took it without investigating any further.

It wasn't until a day or two later that I had a moment to look inside and what I found surprised me—stamps from all over the world during WWII. I eventually sold the contents of that album on eBay for a significant profit.

Similarly, we may not look too special on the outside, but what God has placed in us is where the real value exists. Second Timothy 2:20-21 states:

> But in a great house there are not only vessels of gold and silver, but also of wood and clay, some for honor and some

for dishonor. Therefore if anyone cleanses himself from the latter, he will be a vessel for honor, sanctified and useful for the Master, prepared for every good work.

A vessel exists to serve a specific purpose for its owner. As believers, we have the choice to be vessels for honor or vessels for dishonor, but notice it's the vessel for honor that is actually useful to the Master. Consider also that the primary purpose of a vessel is to contain or hold something. What do we hold of extremely significant value? We hold the gospel! God has chosen to place His glory and His message of salvation in simple human vessels. Why? God wants people to look into our lives and be attracted to the contents, not the packaging.

Today, rejoice in the knowledge that the Lord uses imperfect vessels because they bring Him the most glory! If the vessel was perfect it would bring glory to the vessel. Instead, God chooses to use us to be the instruments by which He conveys the message of the gospel. So proudly proclaim the gospel message today! Share that beautiful treasure with everyone around you. In doing so, we are like that tattered stamp album with treasure inside!

Day 72—Special Words

As a parent, one of my joys was to have special words, phrases, or even songs that I shared with my children when they were young. Most of them had to do with experiences or memories that we all shared as a family. For example, one of our favorite songs to sing together was the "Best Friend Monkey Club Song" and our favorite way to cool off on a hot day was to have a drink of some "cold best friend water, which must be super cold and super best friend"— you get the idea! To the unknowing observer these statements or songs would be difficult to comprehend, but in our family they reflected the existing love and bond that we share together. Going back even further, when my children were babies, they didn't have a clue what we were saying, but what they did understand was how such words made them feel—closer to Daddy.

There is nothing in the world quite like the gift of tongues, but it does remind me of the "secret language" I shared with my children, especially back in the days when they were too little to comprehend the words being spoken. Tongues can be a very intimate experience we share with the Lord. It can enhance our personal prayer times, bring comfort and peace, and it focuses our mind on the things of the Spirit and eternity. First Corinthians 14:2 says, "For he who speaks in a tongue does not speak to men but to God."

Tongues may be given to us in times when we are overwhelmed with the awesomeness and majesty of God, in times of spiritual warfare and trials when we are literally at the end of ourselves and beyond words that we can articulate, and everything in between. That's why Paul states, "For if I pray in a tongue, my spirit prays, but my understanding is unfruitful. What is the conclusion then? I will pray with the spirit, and I will also pray with the understanding" (1 Corinthians 14:14-15). I like how Paul says, "I will pray." Whether it was in the spirit with tongues he did not understand or in a known language he did understand, either way he was committed to pray.

Perhaps you have been confused, misinformed, or even fearful of the gift of tongues. Let go of those burdens today and remember that your Heavenly Father only gives good and perfect gifts. If the Spirit has placed it on your heart to desire the gift of tongues, ask for it with boldness! Trust that if you need it, the Lord will grant it. If He doesn't, then be at peace with His decision. Regardless, let the fear of the unknown be left behind you and instead move forward with eager expectation for all the marvelous works that God wants to do in and through your life. Special words are just the beginning!

Day 73—Don't Lose Heart

Life can certainly be tough and there are plenty of opportunities for us to be overwhelmed by our circumstances. A common one for me is when I am working around the house and a simple project suddenly becomes much more complicated. I remember at our first home there was this huge juniper bush that had grown around the lamppost by the front gate. I thought the juniper was ugly, so I decided to remove it. I had removed about half of it when the lamppost suddenly fell over! It turned out that the lamppost was never actually secured to the ground, it was just propped up by the juniper. So what started off as a simple landscape improvement became a concrete and electrical project, too! I was pretty frustrated and discouraged. In the end, I learned that mixing a batch of concrete and swapping out a light fixture are actually pretty useful things for a homeowner to know and I have used that knowledge many times since.

Christians are still human and we are certainly not impervious to discouragement, especially when it comes to struggles or suffering because we are living to please and honor God. Paul encourages us when he writes in Galatians 6:7-9:

> Do not be deceived, God is not mocked;
> for whatever a man sows, that he will

also reap. For he who sows to his flesh will of the flesh reap corruption, but he who sows to the Spirit will of the Spirit reap everlasting life. And let us not grow weary while doing good, for in due season we shall reap if we do not lose heart.

As Christians, filled and empowered with the Holy Spirit, we have a new perspective, a different outlook, and an unending power source through the Spirit. What might seem like dire circumstances to the world is, for the believer, another opportunity to witness the Lord's faithfulness and grace. God's people have every reason not to lose heart or burn out because we have the Holy Spirit fueling and sustaining us.

Our enemy attempts to deceive us constantly concerning our circumstances. He wants to see us beaten down, discouraged, and burned out—but we have a choice! We can choose to either relinquish authority over our mind and emotions to the enemy—of which Satan has no valid claim—and as a result live our lives in a perpetual state of defeat, or we can choose to stand on the promises of God! Today, let's choose to reject the lies and instead claim God's assurances. God's Word guarantees us, "we shall reap if we do not lose heart." That's a promise we can bank on!

Day 74—Discern Me This

Some years ago, I was job hunting and I came across a seemingly incredible opportunity. I applied on a whim and ended up landing the job. All seemed well initially, but by the end of the first week I felt a check in my spirit that something was wrong. I chocked it up to new job jitters, but by the end of the second week I was sure something was definitely wrong. Although nothing seemed out of place on the surface, I strongly sensed that the Lord was telling me to leave. In truth, the Lord had never given me the green light to accept the job, but He was definitely telling me to step away. It has never been my style to suddenly quit a job after only two weeks, but I obeyed in faith.

Then a few years later, a news article caught my eye. That same company I briefly worked for was now under investigation by multiple law enforcement agencies for all kinds of fraud-related illegal activity—all of which took place *after* I left. On the surface everything looked alright, but in the spiritual realm sin was being birthed and so God used discernment to warn me.

The gift of discernment is a supernatural insight into the spiritual realm. In Acts 8:13-24, we read the account of Peter manifesting the gift of discernment when he revealed that Simon had a heart that desired supernatural power for all the wrong reasons. Simon offered the apostles money in exchange for the power of the Holy Spirit, to which Peter responded, "your heart is not right in the sight of God…For I see that you are poisoned by bitterness and bound by iniquity" (Acts 8:21 and 23).

On the surface, Simon appeared to be on the right track. According to verse 13 he believed, was baptized, and continued with the apostle Philip, but there was still a spiritual heart issue going on behind the scenes and God granted Peter the gift of discernment (as well as a few other gifts) to expose Simon and give him the opportunity to get his heart right. In doing so, God protected His infant church from corrupt intentions.

That is what the gift of discernment does—it protects us (and others) by allowing us to discern things in the spiritual realm. Have you ever felt a check in your spirit or an unexplained uneasiness regarding a person or situation that you just couldn't quite put your finger on or explain? That may very well have been the Lord using the gift of discernment to warn you. Today, let's pray that God would give us both wisdom and clarity to be sensitively attuned to the Holy Spirit that we might accurately discern what is of His kingdom and what is not, and how we should proceed with that information.

Day 75—Letters of Our Lives

I remember when I attended a men's retreat in Ouray, Colorado. While I was there I found a letter my daughter, Skylar, who was eight at the time, had snuck into my duffle bag. She has always been artistic, so the letter was full of drawings. One drawing showed me sleeping in a tent and staring at a full moon, while she was sleeping in her own bed back at home and staring at the same moon. Another drawing showed us both standing side-by-side, holding hands. I wish I could show you what the letter looks like because it truly is precious. She also wrote that she missed me and loved me. Of course, I already knew that, but the drawings and the words of her letter to me were tangible evidence of what I knew in my heart.

In Second Corinthians 3:2-3, Paul references evidence of God's tangible work in the Corinthian church by describing them as a letter, when he writes:

> You are our epistle written in our hearts,
> known and read by all men; clearly you
> are an epistle of Christ, ministered by us,
> written not with ink but by the Spirit of
> the living God, not on tablets of stone but
> on tablets of flesh, that is, of the heart.

In looking at the lives of the church of Corinth, Paul could attest that he was the pen, their hearts were the paper, the Holy Spirit was the ink, and the author was Jesus Christ! In other words, the fruit that was taking place in their lives was evidence that Paul's ministry to them was authentic; they were living, breathing letters of commendation that Paul was being used as an instrument in the hands of God.

Just like my daughter's precious letter to me is evidence of her love for me, so our changed lives and hearts are letters of evidence of God's handiwork, too. I can take Skylar's letter and show it to everyone as proof that what she wrote to me is true. Similarly, our lives are letters that can be read by everyone as well. When people read us, do they see the work of the Holy Spirit in our lives and hearts? Do they read letters of lives transformed and changed by the healing and redemptive power of Jesus Christ's love and grace? Let's take a prayerful moment today to consider what the letters of our lives proclaim!

Day 76—God Wants to Tell You Something

When my brother, Eddie, was fifteen years old, he was in a major car accident that nearly killed him. His back was broken and his intestines ruptured. After multiple surgeries and nearly a month in the Intensive Care Unit he was on the road to recovery, but his promising football career was over. Eddie spiraled downward into a world of alcohol and drugs, all while blaming God for what happened to him.

For many years he lived that lifestyle, hitting rock bottom over and over again. Our parents were at the end of themselves, certain that any day we would get news of Eddie's death. Despite what was obviously happening, God revealed to me that Eddie would one day repent and eventually he would be a pastor. That was a hard sell to tell my parents when they were in the midst of their heartbreak, but praise God, Eddie is now clean and sober, he's an ordained pastor, and he now lives in Texas where he has planted a church.

God will often use prophecy to speak of future events. It's just one of the ways we see Him active and involved in the details of our lives. Consider how the Lord used Agabus, in Acts 21:10-11, to warn Paul of his impending arrest in Jerusalem:

> And as we stayed many days, a certain prophet named Agabus came down from

Judea. When he had come to us, he took Paul's belt, bound his own hands and feet, and said, "Thus says the Holy Spirit, 'So shall the Jews at Jerusalem bind the man who owns this belt, and deliver him into the hands of the Gentiles.'"

Now, this may not seem like the kind of prophecy any of us would want to hear, but I admire how Paul responds in verse 13, when he says, "I am ready not only to be bound, but also to die at Jerusalem for the name of the Lord Jesus." Paul received Agabus' prophecy as authentic, and sure enough it came true. The Lord used Agabus to prepare Paul for what was to come.

You might be thinking, *I've never received nor given a prophecy before.* May I humbly and lovingly challenge you that perhaps you aren't looking through the proper lens? Today, I pray that God would grant us all the ability to see the events of our lives through spiritual, not natural, eyes. I assure you, the Spirit is at work all around and through us! The gift of prophecy is alive and well, and active. We just need to have a heart of faith and discernment to know it when we hear it. So pay close attention today…God wants to tell you something!

Day 77—Skilled and Innocent

The summer that I worked at a Christian camp in Idyllwild, CA I met and befriended an incredibly anointed group of young people who would spend that summer working alongside me. I'll never forget how we bonded the very first weekend and then spent the next two months experiencing life together. It was a tough goodbye when the summer was over and it was time for everyone to head back home. The Holy Spirit had moved powerfully in and through each individual up on that mountain. It was an amazing experience and it changed my life.

Sadly, it wasn't long after we all arrived home that I began to see a change in my friends from camp. Many began experimenting with sin, testing boundaries in a curiosity that would ultimately destroy the unity that the group once shared. There was an innocence that was lost and it broke my heart to watch it happen.

In Romans 16:19, Paul writes, "I want you to be wise in what is good, and simple concerning evil." The Greek word for "wise" in this verse is *sophos,* which means someone who is "skilled" or an "expert." Likewise, the word for "simple" is *akeraios*, which can be translated "innocent." Paul is saying that in order for us to guard ourselves against those elements which would deceive and divide us as believers, we should become experts in what is good and innocent concerning evil.

Think about that—innocent concerning evil. Sometimes, Christians are deceived into believing the best way to overcome sin is to be exposed to it. This is a lie from the enemy. As that group from Idyllwild learned, playing with fire only gets you burned. Exposure to sin is not the way to overcome sin; instead, becoming skilled in righteousness based on an abiding relationship with Jesus Christ is the *only* way to truly be victorious!

I've heard that bankers can spot counterfeit money simply by touching it. Something about it just doesn't "feel" right. The interesting thing is they don't develop this sensitivity by being exposed to counterfeit money, but by being constantly exposed to real money. The principle is the same spiritually. When we are skilled in righteousness, not only will we be innocent concerning evil, but we will be in a stronger position to recognize and avoid sin.

Jesus said in Matthew 10:16, "Behold, I send you out as sheep in the midst of wolves. Therefore be wise as serpents and harmless as doves." May we be a people who refuse to succumb to sin, taking captive every unrighteous curiosity, and seek to be skilled in the way of righteousness!

Day 78—It's Not About Us

Starting a business from scratch is not for the faint of heart, especially in real estate in 2007 right as the housing bubble burst and the Great Recession hit! One day, I was meeting in the office of a good friend of mine, who is a hardworking, successful, godly businessman, and I was sharing with him the precarious position we were in financially. In the middle of the conversation he excused himself for a few minutes and left me in his office. When he returned a short while later he handed me a check for $1,000! He told me this was not a loan, it was a gift to be used to pay our bills that month. His real estate business was also being adversely affected by the economy; yet, he sacrificed to help me in my time of need. I was humbled and left speechless by his act of selflessness.

We see this call to selflessness in Romans 14:7, when Paul reminds us, "For none of us lives to himself, and no one dies to himself." Earlier in the chapter, we see that when a matter is a "nonessential" issue there is liberty to pursue convictions that we may feel led to follow. However, our motivation in doing so should not be based on self-centeredness. Whether we acknowledge this truth or not, none of us as followers of Christ exist in an isolated vacuum. We are all integral members of the body of Christ and we must always place the interests of the body above our own. Therefore, we should not allow our convictions to be about ourselves.

We see this principle all throughout scripture. Philippians 2:3 exhorts, "Let nothing be done through selfish ambition or conceit, but in lowliness of mind let each esteem others better than himself." Romans 12:10 says, "Be kindly affectionate to one another with brotherly love, in honor giving preference to one another."

Regarding our convictions on debatable matters, we need to ask ourselves a few questions and we must answer honestly. Is this conviction inspired by the Holy Spirit or an emotion? Does this conviction cause the body of Christ to be strengthened or to stumble? Does this conviction draw us closer to God or does it feed our flesh? Finally, does this conviction draw attention to Jesus Christ or to us?

I think we would all agree that self-centeredness is an undesirable quality; yet, as human beings, we are all susceptible to such behavior. That's why it is such a powerful testimony when we live selflessly. Paul wrote in Philippians 2:5, "Let this mind be in you which was also in Christ Jesus." We are to follow the example of our risen Savior and put other people's needs above our own. When we do so, we walk in the footsteps of our Lord, and in the process, we honor and glorify the name of Jesus Christ.

Day 79—Ignorant No More

When I first started my transition into full-time vocational ministry, I also worked part-time in the clubhouse at Forest Home Christian camp, which was a major blessing, but it also reminded me of how much I don't know about cooking. Granted, I was the new guy, but on my first shift I sure made some rookie mistakes. Praise God, all my mistakes were easily corrected by the shift leader (who was a teenager), but I still felt bad. As a result of my lack of knowledge, I was limited in the quality and quantity of my work. My effectiveness was hampered by my ignorance. The good thing is that as my shortcomings were revealed, I had an opportunity to choose to learn and grow, or to remain in that state of ineffectiveness. I wanted to learn more so I could be more effective for the kingdom and to bring God greater glory!

In a similar fashion, Paul writes in First Corinthians 12:1, "Now concerning spiritual gifts, brethren, I do not want you to be ignorant." Ignorance is not a quality that looks good on believers, especially when it comes to the gifts that the Holy Spirit graces us with. Paul exhorts in First Timothy 4:14, "Do not neglect the gift that is in you." For us not to neglect our gifts, we first must know what they are, and I believe that God does want us to know. After all, it's God's desire that the gifts be used "for the equipping of the saints for the work of ministry, for the edifying of the body of Christ" (Ephesians 4:12). If we choose to remain ignorant concerning our spiritual gifts, then not only do we miss out on being used fully by Him, but we also won't experience the full potential that God created us for!

Do you want to know what your spiritual gifts are? Then pause reading this devotion right now and pray out to God to reveal them to you. I believe with all my heart that He will honor and answer that sincere prayer. Jesus said in Matthew 7:7-8:

> Ask, and it will be given to you; seek, and you will find; knock, and it will be opened to you. For everyone who asks receives, and he who seeks finds, and to him who knocks it will be opened.

God does not want us to be ignorant of His truth. In fact, Jesus proclaimed in John 8:32, "And you shall know the truth, and the truth shall make you free." Jesus came to bring us truth—He IS truth—and there is freedom in the truth that God reveals. So let's embrace His truth and be free to seek and use our spiritual gifts for His kingdom and for His glory!

Day 80—In the Name of Love

Have you ever had a difficult neighbor? Growing up, we had really interesting neighbors. There were always parties, loud music, police raids—you name it! Law enforcement even informed my parents that the neighbors' eldest son, Luis, was a suspected gang member.

One day, the doorbell rang and when my mom looked through the peephole she saw Luis standing on the other side. She felt nervous and scared, but something seemed wrong, so she opened the door. It turned out he was having a severe asthma attack right on her front porch. A 911 call and an ambulance ride later, and my mom's heart was changed. She now saw him with eyes of compassion, and so my parents began to tell him about Jesus.

Love is the key. It's a game changer. Love is such an important ingredient to a healthy Christian life that when Galatians 5:22-23 describes the fruit of the Spirit, the first one listed is love. "But the fruit of the Spirit is love, joy, peace, longsuffering, kindness, goodness, faithfulness, gentleness, self-control. Against such there is no law." It is a Spirit-led love that results in us cultivating the rest of the fruit.

After stating that the greatest commandment of all is to love God, Jesus continues in Matthew 22:39-40 with the second greatest commandment, which is,

"'You shall love your neighbor as yourself.' On these two commandments hang all the Law and the Prophets." How so? Because as Paul points out in Romans 13:10, "Love does no harm to a neighbor; therefore love is the fulfillment of the law." In verse 8, Paul says the same thing, "he who loves another has fulfilled the law."

When we show love to others—genuine, godly, Spirit-led love—then whether we plan to or not, the law is obeyed. We won't commit adultery, murder, steal, bear false witness, or covet when we love someone. Love does not harm. Therefore, when we love people, the law is fulfilled. That's how amazing love is!

Four months after my mom's experience with Luis, he had a second severe asthma attack and ended up brain dead on life support. I don't know for certain where he stood with the Lord, but I do know this, for four months Luis heard and experienced the love of Christ through my parents. The love of God is powerful, it changes lives, and it turns the world upside-down. As children of God, we have that love in us. So who will we share it with today?

Day 81—Family for the Better

We've all known people who were a bad influence in our lives. I remember being eighteen years old and hanging out with some worldly Christian friends in a shopping center parking lot. There was a shopping cart from the local grocery store nearby and one of my friends challenged me to get into the cart and let him push me with his car. Foolishly, I agreed. It was all laughs until suddenly, like a cartoon character strapped to a rocket, I was thrown back as the car quickly accelerated. I looked behind me and saw a maniacal expression on my supposed friend's face. We were headed straight for a building on the opposite end of the parking lot!

I knew I had to either jump out of the shopping cart or plow headlong into the building. Neither option was good, but at least I had a chance if I jumped—so I did. I remember rolling, the car blowing past (barely missing me), the brakes screeching, and the empty shopping cart slamming into the building so hard it bounced off and somersaulted in the air.

As Christians, we expect the world to be a negative influence, but it's harder to comprehend Christians poorly influencing each other, too. Sadly, this is entirely possible. One of my favorite scriptures is Proverbs 27:17, which says, "As iron sharpens iron, so a man sharpens the countenance of his friend." I've always considered this verse to be a good example of what a God-honoring relationship should look like. Does the interaction of both individuals positively sharpen one another, or do they dull one another instead? I believe it's clear that God's heart is that His children would be a sharpening influence in each other's lives. We see the Lord's heart in Hebrews 10:24-25, which states:

> And let us consider one another in order to stir up love and good works, not forsaking the assembling of ourselves together, as is the manner of some, but exhorting one another, and so much the more as you see the Day approaching.

Today, let's purpose in our hearts to ditch any negativity, division, gossip, or backstabbing, and instead choose to stir each other up for love and good works. Christ died on the cross to free us from bondage! Why would we willingly choose to enslave ourselves again? Or perhaps you've been hurt in the past by a brother or sister in Christ and you're avoiding church. Don't run away, don't give the enemy a foothold; instead, remember the grace Christ extended to you and embrace the gathering of the body of Christ. We're all going to spend eternity together anyway…and eternity begins now!

Day 82—Cast Off That Sweater Vest

One year for Easter, I decided to wear a sweater vest that had been sitting in my closet for a couple of years. I had been waiting for the right opportunity to wear it and so I decided that Sunday morning was the day! Now this may be a stretch, but perhaps when I first came into possession of the sweater vest it might have been in style. I emphasize the word "might." Regardless, for the remainder of the day I endured much good-natured mocking and teasing from my closest friends. There were many "Carlton" jokes and much singing of the Tom Jones classic, "It's Not Unusual" (if you're familiar with the '90s sitcom *The Fresh Prince of Bel-Air* you get the joke). Don't get me wrong, I had a ton of laughs at my own expense and it was a super fun day, but by the end of it I couldn't wait to take off that sweater vest and toss it in the trash!

We all know the sensation of wanting desperately to get an article of clothing off of us, to cast it away from us as quickly as possible. It is with this urgency in mind that Paul wrote in Romans 13:12, "The night is far spent, the day is at hand. Therefore let us cast off the works of darkness." The Greek phrase for "cast off" can also be translated, "to put off or put away," like a piece of clothing. The idea is that works of darkness are inappropriate attire for followers of Christ. When our clothing is dirty, stained, worn out, or like my sweater vest, just plain outdated, we don't continue wearing it! Instead, we take those clothes off in order to put on something much better. In the same way, we are to take off the clothing of darkness and sin, so that we can put on a better covering— Jesus!

Notice the sense of urgency in verse 12—"the day is at hand." If you've ever stayed up all night or been awake while it was still dark outside, you've seen the exact moment when the night is ending and the day is about to dawn. You can sense that time is running out for the night. There is a change in the air as the rays of the sun begin to shine over the horizon and the darkness fades away. Paul is reminding us there is not a moment to be wasted because the true Son is about to rise in the sky. Jesus Christ will be returning soon to claim His bride, the church, and we need to be dressed appropriately!

So let's cease being distracted by the things of this world. Let's cast off with enthusiasm and urgency the works of sin and darkness. How can we do this? Galatians 5:16 says, "Walk in the Spirit, and you shall not fulfill the lust of the flesh." Our salvation is near, the dark night is almost over, our Savior is coming, it's time to wake up and get dressed. So cast off that ugly sweater vest of sin and toss it in the trash once and for all!

Day 83—Why Do I Have to Clean My Room?

Like many children, my bedroom was a mess with clothes and toys strewn everywhere. My closet was the worst of all. Everything in my closet was literally held inside by the door. Opening the door was like popping a trap—everything would come pouring out! This eventually ended one weekend when I was invited to go to a friend's birthday party and my parents wouldn't let me go until I cleaned my room.

It took me the entire weekend to clean it all and when I was finally done (just in time for school on Monday), I vowed I would never again lose an entire weekend cleaning my room. From that day on, I kept my room orderly, which had two positive outcomes: first, I was honoring my parents by submitting to their authority in keeping my room clean, and second, cleaning my room daily made it much easier to keep it that way! I still try to maintain that habit, even now as an adult.

Scripture teaches us that our Heavenly Father is a God of order. In fact, you could say that order is a character trait that reflects the divine nature. First Corinthians 14:33 proclaims, "For God is not the author of confusion but of peace." In other words, there is a method and an order to everything that the Lord does.

The basis of the order that God has established always has to do with coming under authority. For example, First Corinthians 11:3 states, "But I want you to know that the head of every man is Christ, the head of woman is man, and the head of Christ is God." Here we see a systematic order for authority with respect to our worship within the church. God has established order in the universe, government, church, family, and even our lives. First Corinthians 14:40 says, "Let all things be done decently and in order." Notice, the text says "all things."

Our God is a God of order and Paul reminds us in First Corinthians 11:1, "Imitate me, just as I also imitate Christ." As Christians, we are to imitate the example that God has set for us. God's order always comes back to the issue of coming under authority, which requires our humility. Humility is the very example Christ set before us and that's the example we should follow.

Just like a child coming under the authority of his parents to keep his room clean, we are to humbly come under the authority of our Lord and submit to the order He has established! We may not always understand it…but it is always for our own good.

Day 84—Bad Boys, Bad Boys

I will never forget Halloween night 2001, when we suddenly heard a loud crash out on the street in front of our house. I was about to go outside to investigate when I noticed there were already blue and red lights flashing on the wall. I opened the door and was shocked to find five police cars parked out front, one mangled bicycle, a broken tail light on my pickup, and a grown man wearing a monster costume crying on the curb. What was going on?

Apparently, the guy's girlfriend had just broken up with him so he got drunk, hopped on his bicycle, and went to her house in a costume to scare her—so she called the police. When the police showed up he tried to outrun them *on his bicycle* and promptly crashed head-on into my parked pickup truck. When they found drugs in his pocket, he started to wail, "Oh man, don't tell my grandma! She's gonna kill me!" As he was being arrested, one of the police officers asked me if I wanted to press charges against him. "It's all right," I said. "His girlfriend broke up with him, his bicycle is totaled, he's being arrested for drug possession and DUI, and he has to face the wrath of his grandma. He's already in enough trouble as it is!"

Praise God for the police because whether they realize it or not, they are God's ministers, ordained to watch over those who are made in His image. Paul states in Romans 13:4:

> For he is God's minister to you for good. But if you do evil, be afraid; for he does not bear the sword in vain; for he is God's minister, an avenger to execute wrath on him who practices evil.

The Greek word for "minister" in verse 4 is *diakonos*, which is the same word used to describe the servant of a king. Twice in this verse, Paul reminds us the authorities are God's ministers—servants of the King! As such, they are His avengers on those who practice evil. The Greek word for "avenger" is *ekdikos*, which can also be translated, "punisher."

For those who represent the governing authorities, remember that your power doesn't come from the government, or even the people; rather, your authority comes from God, so be just and wise in your application of that power, for you will be held accountable for how you wield it. And for those who are the governed, never forget to show the proper respect for those who are in authority, whether or not they are believers. "For there is no authority except from God, and the authorities that exist are appointed by God" (Romans 13:1).

Day 85—Fleeing Indiana Jones

I remember the very first time I went to Disneyland with my wife, Juanita. It was late in the evening and we decided to get on the Indiana Jones ride before we went home. If you know the ride, the line is interactive and very detailed. No one else was in line with us, so we had freedom to explore at our leisure. There is a section of the line where you are in a narrow hallway and there are some wood beams that appear to be holding up the ceiling. One of those beams, if you shake it really hard, will make a loud crashing sound and the ceiling appears to cave in. I had been on the ride before, but Juanita had not. I wanted to surprise her, so when we got to that part of the line I called her over and quickly shook the wood beam. The room was filled with a loud crash as the ceiling began caving in right over us. With a smile on my face, I turned to see Juanita's reaction, but she was nowhere to be found. She had fled the scene, bailed out on me, jumped ship—call it whatever you want, but she was gone!

To this day, we still laugh at the memory of her fleeing Indiana Jones. Juanita fled first and asked questions later, and that is a perfect illustration of what our reaction toward sexual sin should be. Second Timothy 2:22 says, *"Flee also youthful lusts."* The Greek word for "flee" is *pheugo*, which can also be translated, "to vanish." When the opportunity for sexual sin presents itself to us, we need to vanish, we need to disappear, we need to get as far away as possible and not look back!

In our increasingly sexually permissive society, people have been deceived into believing that actively avoiding sexual sin is extreme and outdated. Yet oddly enough, people have no problem exercising a greater level of caution over far less serious threats.

As Christians, we know that sexual sin defiles the body which is the temple of the Holy Spirit, it contaminates us with the sin of rebellion against God's holy plans, it creates a oneness between two people that should not be, and it brings a slew of emotional, spiritual, and physical consequences. First Thessalonians 4:3-5 states:

> For this is the will of God, your sanctification: that you should abstain from sexual immorality; that each of you should know how to possess his own vessel in sanctification and honor, not in passion of lust.

God's Word and His will are clear. So, is fleeing sexual sin extreme and outdated? No way. In fact, it's kind of like fleeing Indiana Jones—it's better to be safe than sorry.

Day 86—Surrender

Most of us have had a car break down at the most inopportune moment. I remember this one time our car drove fine to the church office, but a few hours later when it was time to go home, I found myself broken down in a rainy parking lot with the gear shift stuck in the "park" position. For nearly an hour, I tried to get the car into a different gear, but it just would not budge. I also couldn't figure out how to close the sunroof, so the rain was pelting me on my head! Needless to say, I was not pleased. In frustration I thought, *Why won't the car surrender?*

It reminded me that as followers of Jesus Christ, we are called to surrender. Romans 12:1 says, "I beseech you therefore, brethren, by the mercies of God, that you present your bodies a living sacrifice." Each day, we are called to lay our "self" down on the altar, as we surrender to the will of God in our lives. We must lay down our selfish ambitions, goals, dreams, desires—everything! Like Paul, we are now bondservants of Christ, having been purchased with His blood.

Just like a broken down car resists the will of its owner, our natural pride, our flesh, often resists Christ's lordship in our lives. It's a constant battle. Yet, scripture makes God's will clear for us. Our mindset should be one of humility and surrender. Just like John the Baptist proclaimed in John 3:30, "He must increase, but I must decrease." Jesus said it best in Luke 9:23 when He stated, "If anyone desires to come after Me, let him deny himself, and take up his cross daily, and follow Me." The cross is a place of surrender and sacrifice, and so as disciples of Christ, we too have a cross to bear.

So what happens when we decrease, when we deny ourselves, when we take up our cross daily, when we lay ourselves down as a living sacrifice? We find life—the sweetest, most joyful, abundant living that we could ever possibly imagine! Right after Jesus tells us to take up our cross in verse 23, He promises in Luke 9:24, "For whoever desires to save his life will lose it, but whoever loses his life for My sake will save it." When we become a living sacrifice, when we die to "self," God brings us into a newness of life like nothing we have ever experienced.

It's funny, a broken down car which won't surrender can only sit in the garage, unused and immobile, not fulfilling the purpose for its existence. That can be a picture of us if we refuse to surrender to our Lord. Don't settle for an existence like a busted up car sitting in the garage. Instead, let's surrender to Jesus, taking up our cross daily as a living sacrifice, and choose life!

Day 87—Doing Laundry

I was a newly minted freshman in high school when my parents decided I was now old enough to do my own laundry. I had watched my mom do it countless times, so when she asked me if I needed any instruction, I firmly told her "no." Exuberantly embracing my new responsibility in life, I proceeded to take a large stack of my dark colored, brand new school clothes and wash them on my own. I poured in the liquid detergent, softener...and then bleach. I was so proud of myself, until I opened the washing machine to transfer the clothes into the dryer. To my complete horror, all my new school clothes were covered in bleach spots! Clearly, I had no idea how to properly wash laundry.

Fortunately, when it comes to washing lives, no one can do what Jesus can! First Corinthians 6:11 tells us, "But you were washed, but you were sanctified, but you were justified in the name of the Lord Jesus and by the Spirit of our God." The Greek word for "washed" is *apolouo*, which means, "to wash off or away." This conveys the idea that we weren't just washed, but that in the process of washing, something was actually removed from us. What was removed? The stain of sin.

Isaiah 1:18 states, "Though your sins are like scarlet, they shall be as white as snow; though they are red like crimson, they shall be as wool." God has washed us with the blood of His Son, Jesus Christ, and as believers, we are now completely clean!

Of course, this isn't what Satan wants us to believe. He wants to lead us into self-condemnation and uncertainty about our salvation. The enemy loves to remind us of all our shortcomings, flaws, and weaknesses. He revels in rubbing our faces in our past sins. Yet, in Psalm 103:10 and 12, David tells us that God "has not dealt with us according to our sins, nor punished us according to our iniquities...as far as the east is from the west, so far has He removed our transgressions from us."

Today, walk forward in boldness and confidence in the work that Jesus Christ completed on the cross. He cleansed us and washed away the filthy stain of sin from our lives, and clothed us in His own righteousness instead. As a result, God "delivered us from the power of darkness and conveyed us into the kingdom of the Son of His love, in whom we have redemption through His blood, the forgiveness of sins" (Colossians 1:13-14).

Day 88—Who Ate All the Chips?

Whenever I look back on my childhood, I always end up laughing because of all the funny memories I shared with my siblings. For example, one thing that used to drive me crazy, but is hilarious to me now, was my younger brother's definition of "sharing" food. When Eddie was a little kid, if my parents bought a bag of potato chips and Eddie got to them first, they would say, "Be sure to leave some for your brother and sister." Well, by the time I got to the bag there would be one chip left. I mean that literally—*ONE* chip! Eddie would eat the *entire* bag and then leave only one chip so that technically he obeyed our parents by leaving "some" for the rest of us!

It reminds me of how we sometimes do that to God. Instead of giving Him our first, we give Him our last. Proverbs 3:9 tells us, "Honor the Lord with your possessions, and with the firstfruits of all your increase." In scripture, the "firstfruits" were the first grain of the harvest—the result of God's provision and blessing. By setting aside even the first portion of dough which came from the harvest as an offering, the people were honoring and thanking God by acknowledging that the harvest belonged to Him and was a gift from Him!

Paul states in Romans 11:16, "For if the firstfruit is holy, the lump is also holy." Paul reminds us that when we set aside our firstfruits as an offering to God, He accepts and makes them holy, and in doing so, He then sanctifies what remains. This opens the door to bless the rest of our lives, as Proverbs 3:10 says, "so your barns will be filled with plenty."

Of course, God doesn't need our firstfruits—everything already belongs to Him and comes from Him. Yet, He desires that we offer Him our firstfruits because when we do so, He is able to do a work in us. Giving Him our firstfruits sets everything in the proper perspective: it acknowledges that all provision comes from God alone, it places the emphasis on eternity and not on this earth, it reminds us to deny ourselves, and it stretches our faith.

So let's make a commitment together to honor God with the firstfruits of our finances by tithing first when we get paid, our time by beginning each day in prayer, worship, and studying the Bible, and our energy by serving Him and others before we consider ourselves. In other words, let's stop leaving God with the last chip in the bag and instead, give Him the first one!

Day 89—Bad Ingredients

We all have our strengths and weaknesses, and I am very much aware of my weaknesses. If not for my lovely wife who knows how to whip up a delicious meal, and for fast food (when she isn't around), I would probably go hungry. It's not that I don't want to cook, it's just that I'm not very good at it. Perhaps I have been traumatized by past experiences where I didn't use the right ingredients, or used the wrong measurements—always with disastrous results! Regardless, I know for a fact that one bad ingredient can spoil a good dish. So, when people ask why I don't cook, I just tell them, "I don't cook for people I love." They usually laugh, which makes me laugh because I'm not trying to be funny, I'm being serious!

Have you ever considered how sin is like a bad ingredient in our lives? Paul writes in First Corinthians 5:6-7, "Do you not know that a little leaven leavens the whole lump? Therefore purge out the old leaven, that you may be a new lump, since you truly are unleavened." Leaven was used to make dough rise, like yeast. Because of leaven, a piece of dough would "puff up." It didn't take much, only a pinch to utterly affect the dough it was mixed in. All throughout scripture, the image of leaven is usually associated with sin. In other words, it's an illustration that should not describe the church.

Unleavened bread would certainly be changed if leaven were added to it. Likewise, we, being described as unleavened bread, will also become negatively affected if we do not purge the leaven (sin) out of our lives. Why should this matter so deeply to us? As verse 7 goes on to say, "For indeed Christ, our Passover, was sacrificed for us."

Do those words affect us? Do we get goosebumps when we hear them? Jesus Christ was sacrificed for us! Isaiah 53:5 states, "But He was wounded for our transgressions, He was bruised for our iniquities; the chastisement for our peace was upon Him, and by His stripes we are healed." All glory and honor to our merciful Savior—we are healed!

We are no longer tainted by the leaven of our former sin and we no longer need to be slaves to the leaven of present and future sin; instead, we can choose to walk by the power of the Holy Spirit in holiness and newness of life. The blood of Jesus Christ has purged the leaven of sin from our lives. We are now like a brand new unleavened lump of dough, covered in His perfect righteousness that only He has the authority to impute to us—that is who we truly are in Christ. So today, let's make a decision to remain that way!

Day 90—Transformed Lives

Whenever I contemplate who I was before Jesus Christ radically transformed my life, it always shocks me. Though I know that person is my past, I no longer recognize him. I don't have any relationship or connection with that former version of myself anymore. He might as well be a stranger to me. I don't know him—he died a long time ago! This is the evidence of the power of Jesus Christ to come into a life and utterly and profoundly change it for His glory.

In Romans 11:1, Paul says, "I say then, has God cast away His people? Certainly not! For I also am an Israelite, of the seed of Abraham, of the tribe of Benjamin." Paul reminds the Jews that God is not done with them and he uses his own transformation as proof. Paul was still one of them, yet different because his heart had been transformed by Christ. Paul's lineage was still intact, but his life was no longer the same.

I relate to Paul's words in Galatians 2:20, which proclaims, "I have been crucified with Christ; it is no longer I who live, but Christ lives in me; and the life which I now live in the flesh I live by faith in the Son of God, who loved me and gave Himself for me." I remember the exact moment I submitted to Jesus and offered Him my life. I remember dying to myself and realizing from that point on my life would never be the same. As Second Corinthians 5:17 promises, "Therefore, if anyone is in Christ, he is a new creation; old things have passed away; behold, all things have become new."

Paul was a living example that God was still reaching out to the Jewish people then and we are living examples that God is still reaching out to mankind today! God is not through with Israel and He is not done with us either. Though our lives are transformed, God is still working in and through us. Philippians 1:6 states, "being confident of this very thing, that He who has begun a good work in you will complete it until the day of Jesus Christ."

As we look back on our lives and see the miraculous work that God has done to transform us, our faith is built up and strengthened. So is the faith of those who hear our testimony. It's powerful! This is the reason that Revelation 12:11 says, "And they overcame him [Satan] by the blood of the Lamb and by the word of their testimony." When people hear about my past, they struggle to reconcile it with who I am today. Praise God, that's a good thing! The transformation of our lives is a credit to His love and mercy, not to anything we have done. As the old hymn says, "To God be the glory, great things *He* hath done!"

About the Author

Erik V. Sahakian has committed his life to serving Jesus Christ through teaching God's inerrant Word, ministering to the body of Christ, and writing. He joyfully worships and serves with his wife and children at Wildwood Calvary Chapel in Yucaipa, CA.

43695248R00110

Made in the USA
San Bernardino, CA
23 December 2016